## *Quod scriptura, non iubet vetat*

**The Latin translates, "What is not commanded in scripture, is forbidden:'**

**On the Cover:** Baptists rejoice to hold in common with other evangelicals the main principles of the orthodox Christian faith. However, there are points of difference and these differences are significant. In fact, because these differences arise out of God's revealed will, they are of vital importance. Hence, the barriers of separation between Baptists and others can hardly be considered a trifling matter. To suppose that Baptists are kept apart solely by their views on Baptism or the Lord's Supper is a regrettable misunderstanding. Baptists hold views which distinguish them from Catholics, Congregationalists, Episcopalians, Lutherans, Methodists, Pentecostals, and Presbyterians, and the differences are so great as not only to justify, but to demand, the separate denominational existence of Baptists. Some people think Baptists ought not teach and emphasize their differences but as E.J. Forrester stated in 1893, "Any denomination that has views which justify its separate existence, is bound to promulgate those views. If those views are of sufficient importance to justify a separate existence, they are important enough to create a duty for their promulgation ... the very same reasons which justify the separate existence of any denomination make it the duty of that denomination to teach the distinctive doctrines upon which its separate existence rests." If Baptists have a right to a separate denominational life, it is their duty to propagate their distinctive principles, without which their separate life cannot be justified or maintained.

Many among today's professing Baptists have an agenda to revise the Baptist distinctives and redefine what it means to be a Baptist. Others don't understand why it even matters. The books being reproduced in the *Baptist Distinctives Series* are republished in order that Baptists from the past may state, explain and defend the primary Baptist distinctives as they understood them. It is hoped that this Series will provide a more thorough historical perspective on what it means to be distinctively Baptist.

The Lord Jesus Christ asked, *"And why call ye me, Lord, Lord, and do not the things which I say?"* (Luke 6:46). The immediate context surrounding this question explains what it means to be a true disciple of Christ. Addressing the same issue, Christ's question is meant to show that a confession of discipleship to the Lord Jesus Christ is inconsistent and untrue if it is not accompanied with a corresponding submission to His authoritative commands. Christ's question teaches us that a true recognition of His authority as Lord inevitably includes a submission to the authority of His Word. Hence, with this question Christ has made it forever impossible to separate His authority as King from the authority of His Word. These two principles—the authority of Christ as King and the authority of His Word—are the two most fundamental Baptist distinctives. The first gives rise to the second and out of these two all the other Baptist distinctives emanate. As F.M. Iams wrote in 1894, "Loyalty to Christ as King, manifesting itself in a constant and unswerving obedience to His will as revealed in His written Word, is the real source of all the Baptist distinctives:' In the search for the *primary* Baptist distinctive many have settled on the Lordship of Christ as the most basic distinctive. Strangely, in doing this, some have attempted to separate Christ's Lordship from the authority of Scripture, as if you could embrace Christ's authority without submitting to what He commanded. However, while Christ's Lordship and Kingly authority can be isolated and considered essentially for discussion's sake, we see from Christ's own words in Luke 6:46 that His Lordship is really inseparable from His Word and, with regard to real Christian discipleship, there can be no practical submission to the one without a practical submission to the other.

In the symbol above the Kingly Crown and the Open Bible represent the inseparable truths of Christ's Kingly and Biblical authority. The Crown and Bible graphics are supplemented by three Bible verses (Ecclesiastes 8:4, Matthew 28:18-20, and Luke 6:46) that reiterate and reinforce the inextricable connection between the authority of Christ as King and the authority of His Word. The truths symbolized by these components are further emphasized by the Latin quotation - *quod scriptura, non iubet vetat*— *i.e.,* "What is not commanded in scripture, is forbidden:' This Latin quote has been considered historically as a summary statement of the regulative principle of Scripture. Together these various symbolic components converge to exhibit the two most foundational Baptist Distinctives out of which all the other Baptist Distinctives arise. Consequently, we have chosen this composite symbol as a logo to represent the primary truths set forth in the *Baptist Distinctives Series.*

# CHURCH POLITY:

## OR

## THE KINGDOM OF CHRIST

# CHURCH POLITY:

OR

# THE KINGDOM OF CHRIST

IN ITS

INTERNAL AND EXTERNAL DEVELOPMENT

By

## J. L. REYNOLDS

Pastor of the Second Baptist Church, Richmond, Va.

FIUNT NON NASCUNTUR CHRISTIANI.—Tertul. Apol. 18.

*With a Biographical Sketch of the Author by John Franklin Jones*

RICHMOND, VA.
HARROLD & MURRAY, BROAD STREET.
1849

he Baptist Standard Bearer, Inc.
NUMBER ONE IRON OAKS DRIVE • PARIS, ARKANSAS 72855

Thou hast given a *standard* to them that fear thee;
that it may be displayed because of the truth.
-- Psalm 60:4

*Reprinted 2006*

*by*

## THE BAPTIST STANDARD BEARER, INC.
No. 1 Iron Oaks Drive
Paris, Arkansas 72855
(479) 963-3831

**THE WALDENSIAN EMBLEM**
*lux lucet in tenebris*
"The Light Shineth in the Darkness"

ISBN# 1579785190

# PREFACE.

CHURCH POLITY has become the absorbing topic of the Christian world. In common with all thinking men, I have devoted considerable time to its examination; and have made some progress in the preparation of a volume with the design of exhibiting the polity of the New Testament, and tracing the gradual departures from it in the churches which succeeded those planted by the apostles. The completion of the work, on the plan proposed, will require several years, even under circumstances the most favorable to the prosecution of my labors. Perhaps I may not complete it at all. I have, therefore, yielded the more readily to the suggestion of my worthy friend, the editor of the Periodical Library, to prepare a smaller work, which is now submitted to the public. May the great Shepherd and Bishop of souls bless it to the instruction of the flock, for which he labored and died.

THE AUTHOR.

*Mercer University, July,* 1846.

## PREFACE TO SECOND EDITION.

THE favorable reception with which this little book has met, has encouraged me to prepare a new and enlarged edition, which is now offered to the public, with the hope that it may contribute to the diffusion of correct sentiments on the subject of which it treats.

J. L. REYNOLDS.

*Richmond, August,* 1848.

# CONTENTS

PAGE.

### CHAPTER I.
Statement of the subject, — 1

### CHAPTER II.
Sources of Proof, — 18

### CHAPTER III.
The Church of Christ, — 32

### CHAPTER IV.
Particular Churches, — 49

### CHAPTER V.
A Church, a Single Local Society, — 51

### CHAPTER VI.
Members of a Church, — 56

### CHAPTER VII.
Rights of a Church, — 67

### CHAPTER VIII.
Independence of the Churches, — 98

### CHAPTER IX.
Officers of a Church, — 105

## CHAPTER X.
Identity of Bishops and Elders, - - - - - 119

## CHAPTER XI.
Rights and Duties of Bishops, - - - - 127

## CHAPTER XII.
The Deaconship, - - - - - - - - 134

## CHAPTER XIII.
Ordination, - - - - - - - - 140

## CHAPTER XIV.
Baptism, - - - - - - - - 146

## CHAPTER XV.
The Lord's Supper, - - - - - - - 203

## CHAPTER XVI.
Ralation of Churches to each other. - - - - 212

## CHAPTER XVII.
Advantages of Scriptural Church Polity, - - 218

## CHAPTER XVIII.
Corruption of Scriptural Church Polity, - - - 228

# THE KINGDOM OF CHRIST.

## CHAPTER I.

### STATEMENT OF THE SUBJECT.

When Christ uttered, in the judgment hall of Pilate, the remarkable words — "I am a king,"* he pronounced a sentiment fraught with unspeakable dignity and power. His enemies might deride his pretensions and express their mockery of his claim, by presenting him with a crown of thorns, a reed and a purple robe, and nailing him to the cross; but in the eyes of unfallen intelligences, he was a king. A higher power presided over that derisive ceremony, and converted it into a real coronation. That crown of thorns was indeed the diadem of empire; that purple robe was the badge of royalty; that fragile reed was the symbol of unbounded power; and that cross the throne of dominion which shall never end.

* John 18: 37.

This pregnant truth contained the fulfilment of the hopes which had cheered mankind through all previous generations. When our first parents had broken the covenant, graciously made with them by their Creator, and were expelled from the garden of Paradise, they bore with them the seeds of a glorious promise, which, scattered by their posterity among the nations of the earth, sprung up in the form of a general expectation of a golden age;* and, entrusted to a particular race, inspired them with the confident hope that a deliverer would afterwards arise, who, assuming the position and responsibilities of the second Adam, would arrest the dominion of sin and death, and gather together the covenant people into a kingdom of holiness and love.

The promise which was committed to our first parents, when they traced, with lingering footsteps, the path of their departure from paradise, was entrusted, as a special mark of the divine favor, to Abraham and his seed; and, in its subsequent announcement and corroboration, still further limited to Isaac, to Jacob, and finally to David, who was chosen of God as the favored individual in whose lineage should appear the Lion of the tribe of Judah.

This conception of the Messiah's kingdom was still further developed and amplified by the prophets,

* Hengstenberg's Christology, 1, p. 14–19.

a succession of inspired men, from Samuel to Malachi, who sustained a most important relation to the Jewish Theocracy. While to the priests were committed the direction and support of the ritual service, the external worship of Jehovah, it was the main design of the prophets to cherish and diffuse a theocratic spirit, by which the people might be retained in loyalty to their invisible king. In this elevated sphere were their functions discharged, and to this end were their labors directed. They may thus be considered the forerunners and prototypes of the ministers of the Christian dispensation.\*

In the discharge of their high functions, the prophets announced the coming of the Messiah; predicted the time of his appearance; and, grouping together the most striking and imposing characteristics of earthly sovereignties, presented a magnificent picture of his spiritual kingdom, and of the happiness which the nations would enjoy under his mild and equitable reign. This happy period would be signalized by the restoration of the long lost harmony between Judah and Israel, and the entrance of the

---

\* Der Prophetismus der Hebräer von A. Knobel. Th. I. S. II. Baumgarten-Crusius' Biblische Theologie, § 6, 1. "The primary notion of a prophet," says Stillingfleet, "doth not lie in foretelling future events, but in declaring and interpreting to the world the mind of God, which he receives by immediate revelation from himself." Origines Sacræ, B. II. chap. 5th. Stuart on the O. T. p. 90, note.

Gentiles within the fold of the people of God. The kingdom of the Messiah was not to be limited by geographical divisions, nor restricted to a peculiar nation. The whole world was to be invited to its privileges, and all nations made to share in its blessings.* The most opulent earthly kingdoms had perished, and the most powerful dynasties been destroyed; even Judah and Israel, though blessed with divine protection and guidance, had bowed their necks to the oppressor, and gone into captivity; but the kingdom of the Messiah would never perish, and of his government there would be no end. The uttermost parts of the earth were to be its boundaries, and eternity the measure of its duration.†

When the fulness of the time was come, Jesus of Nazareth appeared, and appropriated these predictions of the Messiah to himself. In striking harmony with the theocratic representations of the prophets, he denominated the dispensation which he introduced, "the kingdom of God, the kingdom of heaven;"‡

---

* Jer. 30: 4, 9; Eze. 37: 24; Hos. 1: 10; Isaiah 11: 10; and Dan. 7: 14.

† Twesten's Dogmatik, I. S. 323. Knapp's Theol. § 91. For a full examination of the Messianic predictions of the O. T. see Hengstenberg's Christology.

‡ The word in the original, which is translated *kingdom*, is equivalent to *kingly authority;* and this expression, modified according to the context, may generally be substituted for it. Dr. Dagg's interpretation of John 3: 5, pp. 9, 23. The expression, *kingdom of heaven*, is a periphrasis for the

and claimed the honor and allegiance due to a divine messenger. Attesting his mission by infallible signs, and declared to be the Son of God with power by his resurrection from the dead, he stood forth, in virtue of his divinity and the appointment of the Father, the head of that spiritual kingdom, of which the Jewish theocracy was but a feeble type.*

The predictions of the prophets and the admoni-

---

*Christian state or dispensation*, and is evidently derived from the mode of thought and speech common to the Jews. "The God Jehovah was their proper king, supreme over their state and nation. He governed them through the instrumentality of human regents and deputed kings.

Their constitution was *theocratic*, to make use of a happy term, first applied to the subject by Josephus. Hence, the Israelitish state and nation are called the *possession*, and *the peculiar people of Jehovah:* as Ex. 19: 6; Psalms 114: 2. In the same way the later Jews applied the phrase, *kingdom of God*, or of *heaven:* vid. Schoettgen, de regno coelorum, (Hor. Heb. T. I. extr.); and Wetstein on Matt. 21: 25." Knapp's Theology, § 99. (1.) vid. Bland on Matt. 3: 2. Campbell on the Gospels, Diss. 5, part 1.

The Lexicons have blundered sadly on this phrase. Tholuck, after an elaborate criticism on Wahl, Bretschneider, and others, gives the following as the true definition: "Christ designates, by 'the kingdom of heaven,' the community of those, who, united through his Spirit under him as the head, rejoice in the truth and enjoy a holy and blissful life; all of which is effected through communion with him." Biblical Repository, I, p. 567. Christian Review, IV., p. 380. Even this is a partial view.

*John 4: 25—26; 9: 35, 37; Matt. 26: 63, 64; 16: 15—17; 27: 11.

tions of Jesus were sufficiently perspicuous to have prevented the formation of erroneous opinions with respect to the nature of this kingdom. Christ declared explicitly that he claimed not to be an earthly monarch; refused to be made king;\* and proved, by many incidents in his life, how little he thought of interfering with the civil concerns of men.† In immediate connection with the assertion of his royalty, he declares that his kingdom is not of this world.‡ And as if to relieve the minds of his disciples of all doubt on the subject, he predicted the destruction of Jerusalem, and the overthrow of the Jewish political state.‖

The history of our race has developed nothing more clearly, than the tenacity with which the mind clings to errors which are sanctioned by universal belief, and hallowed by venerable associations. Notwithstanding our Lord's unambiguous language, with respect to the nature of his kingdom, his followers continued, up to the period of his ascension,§ deeply tinged with the Jewish notion of the Messiah; and few of them rose to the elevated conception of a spiritual economy, which, obliterating all national distinctions, and swaying its sceptre over the souls of men, would dispense to Jew and Gentile alike,

---

\* John 6 : 15.   † Matt. 17 : 24 ; 22 : 21; Luke 12 : 13.
‡ John 18 : 36.   ‖ Luke 19 : 43.   § Acts 1 : 6.

its healing and saving influence. Long after the disciples had attained and promulgated correct views on this subject, the old Judaizing leaven continued to work. A large number of the early professors of christianity, including several distinguished fathers, were persuaded into an expectation of the temporal reign of Christ;\* and Chilaism, although repeatedly convicted of folly and delusion, has subsequently appeared, at intervals, in the history of the Church, and numbered multitudes among the victims of its gross hallucinations. Its latest modern development, Millerism, has just spent its force in our own country.

As the reign of Christ has primary reference to the human race, the Messiah appeared in human form. By his mysterious incarnation, he formed the connecting link between the subjects of his kingdom and himself, allying his divine nature to theirs, and making them partakers of his own. Every real member of Christ's kingdom bears the likeness of its great king. As "the habitation of God through the spirit," the divine and the human are united in him. It is also a necessary inference, from the principle which was stated at the beginning of this paragraph, that the instrumentality by which the kingdom of Christ is promoted among

---

\* Lehrbuch der Dogmengeschichte von Dr. F. H. Meier, § 32.

men must be material as well as spiritual, human as well as divine. These divine and spiritual elements in its organization, are not cognizable by the senses, and must, of course, be invisible. It is only in reference to its human or material elements that it becomes visible. Its local and temporal developments are visible, but its efficient agencies and ultimate ends are spiritual. Wherever the phrases which designate the Messiah's reign, occur in the Scriptures, they refer to it under the one or the other of these aspects. The idea of a visible kingdom of Christ, as embodied in the visible church, is foreign to the letter and spirit of the New Testament.*

The late Dr. Mason, in a work† which is distinguished for the confidence with which he asserts his sentiments, rather than the conclusiveness of his reasoning, or the correctness of his principles of interpretation, maintains that by the kingdom of heaven is designed the "external visible church." "This," he contends, "can be but one, or else it would not be *a* kingdom, and *the* kingdom, but several. And this one must be visible, because its ordinances are administered by visible agency." To

---

* Robinson in his Lexicon, p. 130, has assigned this meaning to the phrase, but the texts he cites fail to establish it.—e. g. Matt. 6: 10, manifestly relates to the spiritual reign of Christ. Schleusner does the same. Pasor is more correct.

† Essays on the Church. New York, 1843, p. 18.

prove his position, the excellent author relies upon several passages of Scripture, particularly those parables in which an analogy is suggested between the kingdom of God and the usages of common life.* His argument is founded upon an erroneous view of the nature and design of a parable, and especially of those which he cites in support of his position. "The parables of the Saviour," as Neander has remarked, "we may define as representations, by which the truths, relating to the kingdom of God, are exhibited in a vivid manner to the eye of the mind, by means of special relations and analogies of common life, whether derived from nature or the world of mankind."† It was no part of his design, in any of them, to present an exact representation of the kingdom of heaven, considered as a unit, but simply to illustrate some particular truth connected with the christian dispensation. To attempt to press the analogy beyond its legitimate limits, and find a specific correspondence between each point in the narrative or fact and the Messiah's kingdom, is contrary to the most approved principles of interpretation. For illustration, it is simply necessary to refer to two parables, which occur in immediate connection with those which Dr. M.

---

\* Matt. 13: 24, 30, 47, 50; 16: 19; 25: 1; 28: 19, 20; John 20: 21, 23.

† Christian Review, vol. 8, p. 202.

has cited. The parables of the mustard seed and of the leaven are intended to represent the diffusiveness of genuine piety, under two different but related aspects. There is but one idea in both of them, though clothed in different drapery, and relating to different forms of development. The former indicates the diffusion of piety, or the extension of the reign of heaven among masses of mankind; the latter refers to the development of the same principle in an individual. There is, therefore, an analogy between the mustard seed and the leaven, on the one hand, and vital religion on the other.

If we proceed to examine the parable of the sower, upon which the author relies with so much confidence, we shall see that it is susceptible of a similar interpretation. It teaches the important truth, that in the progress of the Gospel its pure and legitimate effects would sometimes be mingled with foreign admixtures; that in those organizations which would be established for the propagation of the truth, spurious professors would obtrude themselves among the genuine subjects of his kingdom. Human sagacity could not prevent this conjunction, but a separation would be effected at the end of the world. The parable of the net, to which Dr. M. also refers, teaches the same truth.

Fortunately we are not left to conjecture here. Christ has given his own interpretation of the parable of the sower. He tells us "the field is the world," not the church; and "the children of the kingdom" are distinguished from "the children of the wicked one." If it be urged that these latter are represented in a subsequent verse, as forming a part of his kingdom, since it is said that the angels shall "gather out of his kingdom all things that offend," it is sufficient to reply that the royal authority of Christ extends over his foes as well as his friends. The former may appear in visible connection with his genuine disciples, but have never been recognized by him. Even if this parable were ambiguous, the many passages of Scripture, in which moral and spiritual qualifications are mentioned as indispensable to admittance into the kingdom of the Redeemer, would be sufficient to determine who are his real subjects.*

Great stress is laid, by Dr. M.,† upon the predictions in the Old Testament, in which the kingdom of the Messiah is described. In his judgment they manifestly refer to an external visible community. This view, however, betrays a very imperfect apprehension of the nature of those prophecies, and of just principles of interpretation. He sustains his position only by attaching a literal sense to figurative representations. The passages which he

--------

* Mark 10:15; John 3:3; Col. 1:13; Eph. 5:5; Matt. 3:2; 5:3, &c.
† Pages 8—10.

has quoted are taken from the second part of the book of Isaiah,* one of the most splendid portions of the prophetic writings, in which the prophet, ravished with the glorious vision of the new theocracy, which the Spirit reveals to his mental gaze, portrays it in glowing language, and in imagery derived from the earthly theocracy, or the kingdoms of the earth. A literal interpretation is, here, out of the question. The kingdom which he depicts can be realized only in the spiritual theocracy of the Redeemer. With reference to chap. 60, upon expressions in which Dr. M. relies with great confidence, it may be said, without any assumption of superior perspicacity, in the language of a distinguished critic : — " It can scarcely be necessary to remark, that the whole representation is figurative throughout."† But Dr. M. thinks that " that light, which was to shine upon the Gentiles, and the ' brightness' of that ' rising,' which was to attract the ' kings,' must of necessity be external."—p. 10. But can any one, after even a cursory glance at this chapter, 60, believe that this light is a material, visible light; that the *darkness* which covers the people is its opposite in nature ; and that kings will actually behold this light ? It is clear that the terms are used figuratively — darkness being the

---

\* Isaiah 40–66.

† Hengstenberg's Christology, vol. I, p. 438.

symbol of sin and misery — light, of righteousness and happiness.* The chapter has no reference to a " visible church catholic," but simply describes the extent of the Messiah's reign, and the blessings by which it would be attended.

This kingdom belongs to Christ as Mediator. It differs from his natural kingdom, not in the extent of its sway, but in the authority from which it is derived, and the object for which its government is administered. As God, he possesses an indefeasible right to rule the universe; but as Mediator, he exercises his rule in accordance with the provisions of the covenant of grace, and administers the affairs of his kingdom with special reference to his chosen people.† This kingdom has been committed to him by the Father as the reward of his obedience unto death. As that obedience is possessed of a retrospective efficacy, and delivers from guilt and condemnation the faithful who died before the advent of the Redeemer; so his royal authority, which was first publicly committed to him at his resurrection from the dead, was exercised in the administration

---

\* Rosenmüller thinks the figurative use of these expressions is so evident as scarcely to need notice. Per *lucem* Hierosolymæ oriturum felicem ejus statum significari, uti supra 45: 75, 8: 8, 10, vix monitu opus. Vid. Scholia in V. T. II. p. 747.

† Dick's Theol. Lec. LXIV. Col. 1: 15, 19; Heb. 1: 3, 14.

of his kingdom in every age. His incarnation was only the removal of his audience chamber to earth; the visible manifestation of the divine sovereign; and his ascension to heaven was his public coronation in the sight of the universe.

The benefits of Christ's kingdom are restricted to its real, accredited subjects. But for the purpose of administering its government and promoting its interests, he has been invested with all power in heaven and in earth.\* He sways his sceptre over the armies of heaven, the inhabitants of the earth, and the spirits of hell. All the agents of the universe are held in his hand, and execute his will. All will be made contributors to the promotion of his kingdom, and will grace his final triumph.

The reign of the Redeemer is to be perpetual. Such is the description given of it in ancient prophecy and confirmed by Christ and his apostles.† The only apparent exception to the general tenor of the Scriptures, is found in 1 Cor. 15 : 24, 28. But even this passage, upon a more careful examination, will be found to comport with the representations which are elsewhere found of the perpetual duration of the Messiah's kingdom. The import of this passage seems to be, that God has committed to Christ the

---

\* Matt. 28 : 18; Eph. 1 : 22; John 13 : 3; Phil. 2 : 9, 11; 1 Peter 3 : 22; 1 Cor. 15 : 24, 26.

† Psalm 45 : 6; Heb. 1 : 8; Psalm 72 : 5.

government of his mediatorial kingdom and invested him with full power to carry it on to perfection, by " placing all things under his feet." His enemies oppose his progress in vain ; for he must finally triumph, and put down all opposing " rule, and all authority and power." When this glorious period arrives, he will present the kingdom to his Father, in all the amplitude and splendor of a redeemed and purified possession. His mediatorial work, so far as it regards this world, will be accomplished. He will then see of the travail of his soul, and be satisfied. But lest it should be supposed that he will then abdicate his throne, and resign the authority delegated to him by the Father, the apostle adds— " And when all things shall be subdued unto him, then shall the Son also himself be subject unto him that put all things under him, that God may be all in all." He will still act as the representative of the Father, and administer the government of his kingdom in subservience to the interests and happiness of his redeemed and glorified people.*

* It has been supposed that the phraseology of the 25th verse implies the termination of the reign of Christ. " He must reign *till*, &c." But the word does not necessarily limit the reign of Christ to the event specified, viz : the subjection of his foes. It is said in Romans 5 : 13 —"*Until* the law, sin was in the world." But this does not imply that sin did not exist after the giving of the law. See also parallel expressions in Genesis 28 : 15 ; 1 Samuel 15 : 35 ;

The reign of Christ is a subject of unspeakable dignity and interest. With it are connected the noblest prospects and dearest hopes of mankind. Sages have dreamed of ideal republics; poets have painted the glories of a golden age; and the human race, groaning under the curse of sin, and burdened with the accumulated sorrows of earth, have earnestly longed for a period of respite from grief, and a state of pure and permanent felicity. Under the dominion of the Redeemer, these hopes are fulfilled, these expectations are realized. With the condescension that marks the character of the king, and the unexampled benignity which induced him, at the cost of his own sufferings and death, to rear this kingdom, as an asylum for guilt and a refuge for sorrow, he invites the nations to its rights and immunities. The right of citizenship is proffered, without distinction of clime or country, sex or station. In the distribution of its favors, no regard is had to Jew or Greek, Barbarian or Scythian, bond or free. The possessors of uncertain riches are blessed with spiritual wealth; and the poor are made rich in faith, and heirs of the kingdom of heaven. All its subjects are the sons of God, the redeemed of Christ. Imbued with the graces of heaven, furn-

---

Isaiah 22: 14; Psalms 112: 8; 1 Timothy 4: 13. The passage is similarly interpreted. Biblical Repos. 3, p. 749–755, and Am. Biblical Repos. 2, p. 443.

ished with every thing necessary to their comfort and happiness, and favored with occasional glimpses of the glory in reversion, they possess, even on earth, a joy which is unspeakable, and a peace which passeth all understanding. And when the reign of Christ is fully consummated, and all his followers have entered the heavenly world, they will accede to an inheritance which is as infinite in value, as it is interminable in duration. It is a matter of vast importance, of imperative necessity, to every man that he be a member of this kingdom of Christ. Admittance is granted and the conditions clearly defined. The king himself has inscribed over its portal the solemn words, "Except a man be born again he cannot see the kingdom of God."

# CHAPTER II.

### SOURCES OF PROOF.

As the kingdom of Christ is a subject of pure revelation, it may justly be expected that every thing pertaining to its nature, and to the external organizations by which its principles are to be diffused among men, will be found in the inspired volume, in which that revelation is deposited. But in opposition to this obvious and rational inference, it is asserted by many that the Scriptures contain no specific directions with respect to the outward development of Christ's kingdom—no form of Church government.* If this assumption were correct, if neither Christ nor his apostles had left anything determinate, with respect to the earthly relations of his church, but committed its organization and management entirely to fallible men, we should feel bound humbly to submit to his will, and acquiescing in the wisdom of the arrangement, should do whatever human sagacity and prudence might suggest, to discharge the delicate and momentous trust com-

---

* Hooker Eccl. Pol. B. 3 § 2. § 11. So also Tomline, Paley and other Episcopal divines. Burton's Hist. Church, p. 60. Neander, in Coleman's Prim. Ch. Introduc. p. 18.

mitted to us. But happily for us and for the interests of his kingdom, he has not imposed upon us this fearful responsibility. The Scriptures are a sufficient rule of faith and practice. The principles of ecclesiastical polity are prescribed in them with all necessary comprehensiveness and clearness. The founder of the Church has provided better for its interests, than to commit its affairs to the control of fallible men. "Whatever ways of constituting the church may to us seem fit, proper, and reasonable, the question is, not what constitution of Christ's church seems convenient to human wisdom, but what constitution is actually established by Christ's infinite wisdom."\*

It would have been happy for the world if men had been satisfied with the simple form of ecclesiastical polity contained in the New Testament. Rejecting this, or proceeding upon the assumption that the New Testament contains none, they have attempted to trace analogies between Christ's church and the defunct forms of Judaism, or engrafted upon it rites and ceremonies borrowed from Heathen-

---

\* Edwards's Works, 4, p. 377.

This point is very ably discussed by Dr. Smyth, in his learned works on Presbytery, ch. II., and on Prelacy, Lec. II., Note C. Lec. III., Vid. Dr. Wood's Lectures on Church Government, pp. 9–12. Haldane's View of Social Worship, &c. ch. 2. Milton's Reason of Church Government, ch. I., II.

ism. From the close of the second century down to the present time, a considerable party have derived their notions of ecclesiastical polity from the Jewish temple and priesthood.* And even a late writer has supposed that its rudiments may be discovered in the Jewish sacerdotal institute.† A more gross misconception of the genius of Christianity than is implied in this Judaizing system, can scarcely be imagined. No two persons can be more unlike than a Jewish priest and a Christian minister; and to argue from the prerogatives and duties of the one to those of the other is a gross paralogism.

To model the church of Christ after the Jewish temple is to abjure our liberty in the Gospel, and to relapse into the weak and beggarly elements of Levitical bondage. "To argue from a Levitical priesthood to a Christian ministry, and to prove the validity of the latter institution by an appeal to the former, and specially to compare the official duties of the two respective classes, with an assumption that they are parallel, is out of all question." ‡

---

* Punchard's Hist. of Congregationalism, p. 22. Campbell's Lec. on Eccl. Hist. Lec. X. part I. Gieseler's Church Hist, I. § 65. Mosheim, I. p. 144. Neander, p. 111. Kirchenverfassung von K. D. Hüllmann, S. 35.

† Spiritual Despotism, by Isaac Taylor, Sec. 3.

‡ Stuart on the Old Testament, pp. 88, 388-392. Edwards's Works, IV. pp. 390, 594. Wood's Lectures on Church Government, p. 13. Lord Bacon advised the removal of the offensive term priest from the English Liturgy.

The unscriptural notion of a human priesthood in the church of Christ, is fraught with pestilent error, and has led to the most enormous abuses. It has substituted a new class of mediators between God and man, to the exclusion and dishonor of the one Mediator, the man Christ Jesus; for, as Dr. Arnold has observed, "the essential point in the notion of a priest is this: that he is a person made necessary to our intercourse with God, without being necessary or beneficial to us morally. His interference makes the worshipper neither a wiser man, nor holier than he would have been without it; and yet it is held to be indispensable. This unreasonable, unmoral, unspiritual necessity, is the essence of the idea of priesthood." Viewed in its relations to the cardinal truths of Christianity, no error can be more utterly subversive of the Gospel. We are not, therefore, surprised at the earnestness with which he combats it, and the indignation with which he denounces it, as "the worst and earliest form of Anti-Christ." * It was this human priesthood "bedecked in deformed and fantastic dresses, in palls and mitres, gold and gewgaws, fetched from Aaron's

---

Pacification of the Church, Works I. p. 356. This argument is, in the hands of Prelacy, self-destructive; for the Jewish hierarchy was not prelatical. Smyth's Presbytery, ch. XIII. Taylor's Spiritual Despotism, Sec. 3.

* Arnold on the Church. Miscellaneous Works, pp. 16, 18.

old wardrobe, or the flamen's vestry,"\* that for ages presented Christianity to the world, under the motley image of resuscitated Judaism amalgamating with Paganism. Rearing its colossal throne upon the earth, and stretching its powerful sceptre over the flames of purgatory and the prisons of hell, it robbed life of its last joy, and death of its only hope.

The evils of attempting to graft Christianity upon Judaism, and effect an unnatural amalgamation between carnal ordinances and a spiritual religion, appear, although in a mitigated form, in some of the practices which have crept into use since the age of the apostles. Infant baptism is, in its essential idea, alien to the spirit of Christianity. Whether it be considered the condition, or the privilege of church membership (according to the discrepant views of its supporters), it involves the glaring absurdity of making carnal descent the condition of admittance to spiritual blessings. How futile the effort to effect a coalescence between a right conferred by hereditary transmission and the privileges of a kingdom, in which citizenship is determined by entirely different qualifications, the subjects of which are "born, not of blood, nor of the will of the flesh, nor of the will of man, but of God." "How

---

\* Milton of Reformation in England. Prose Works, p. 1.

unwary are many excellent men," says Prof. Stuart,* "in contending for infant baptism, on the ground of the Jewish analogy of circumcision? Are females not proper subjects of baptism? And again, are a man's slaves to be all baptized because he is? Are they church-members of course, when they are so baptized? Is there no difference between engrafting into a politico-ecclesiastical community, and into one of which it is said that "it is not of this world?"

Where this practice is combined with the priestly dogma of baptismal regeneration, it conduces equally to sacerdotal power and spiritual delusion. Among the great majority of Protestants, its tendency is, to a great extent, neutralized by the assertion of the necessity of the new birth. This salutary truth extracts the poison from the opposite error. Infant baptism possesses no natural affinity for the evangelical scheme. Appended to it, it is a mere heterogeneous addition, which refuses and defies vital incorporation; and its only effect is to mar the heavenly beauty of Christianity by an unnatural and earthly incumbrance. Carnal rites combined with a spiritual religion are as unseemly as would be wings of wax upon the angel Gabriel.

Another class of writers find the original pattern of the Christian church in the polity of the

* Old Testament, p. 395.

synagogue,* and affirm that the Apostles did not introduce new organizations, but converted these Jewish assemblies into Christian churches. A fatal objection to this theory is, that we have not the slightest intimation of it in the New Testament. If it had been the design of the Apostles to present the synagogue as the model of Christian churches, it is incredible that they would have omitted to say so. It may further be urged that the synagogue was not a divine institution,† and could not therefore be adopted as the exemplar of Christian churches, without express divine authority. This authority Christ has not given; the apostles nowhere assert it. We objected to the notion which transfers the Levitical priesthood to the Christian church, that it is a virtual repeal of the Gospel; we object to this scheme, that it exalts a human institution into an

---

* Vid. Vitringa de Synag. et Selden de Synag. Neander's Planting of the Chr. Ch. chap. 2. Gieseler 1. § 25. Whately's Kingdom of Christ, pp. 78–80. Coleman's Prim. Ch. chap. 2. Smyth's Presb. B. 1. ch. 13.

† The divine institution of the synagogue is pleaded by Dr. Smyth and others, from the expression in Psalm 74: 8. "God's synagogues." But at the time this Psalm was composed, synagogues were not in existence. The Hebrew is more properly rendered, "the places of assembly," alluding to Ramah, Bethel, &c., the seats of the prophets (Gesen. Heb. Lex. p. 554); or the plural may be used, as Stuart thinks (O. T. p. 72), for the singular, and the allusion be to the temple.

institution of Christ. Neither of them derives any warrant from the word of God.

We look in vain for the model of a church among the Jews. It was foreign to their modes of conception; nor is there a word in their language by which the idea can be expressed. They had words, or phrases, designating an assembly for religious purposes, and the place or house where such an assembly was convened, but none which embodied the conception of a church as distinguished from a congregation, of an organized body composed of professedly pious persons, professing spiritual qualifications, and combined for the promotion of purely spiritual purposes.* The idea of a church is peculiar to Christianity. "This system presents the only true form of a church. The Jews had no distinct organization which could, with propriety, be denominated a church. Much less is any association under other forms of religion, entitled to this appellation." †

It is well known to all who have examined the subject of ecclesiastical polity, that the testimony of the Fathers has been appealed to as competent authority. But if the Bible be our directory, in

---

\* Josephs, a learned Jew, in his English and Hebrew Lexicon, London, 1834, under the word church, gives phrases which indicate only the house used for religious purposes.

† Coleman's Christian Antiquities, ch. 1, § 3.

faith and practice, why need we apply to other sources for information? Should it be found, upon examination, that the testimony of the Fathers conflicts with the practice of the Apostles, it must be rejected. The form of church government, taught in the Scriptures, must be ascertained, before we can determine how far this testimony is entitled to credit. Upon Protestant and Scriptural principles, no other course is admissible.

The advocates of tradition proceed upon the assumption that the Scriptures do not contain a revelation of all that is necessary for "doctrine, for reproof, for correction, for instruction in righteousness; that the man of God may be perfect, thoroughly furnished unto all good works;" and in support of it they refer to doctrines and practices which have been very generally received, but are not taught or enjoined in the word of God. Thus, Klee, a Roman Catholic, says that "many things in the ethical and liturgical practice of the church are retained which rest only on traditional grounds, as the lawfulness and necessity of infant baptism, the validity of heretical baptism, &c."* When we consider how far the Puseyites have advanced in their approach to Rome, we are not surprised to find

---

*Lehrbuch der Dogmengeschichte, I. S. 114. Compare Hooker's Eccl. Pol. B. I. ch. 14. Townsend's N. T. P. 10. Note 9.

one of them denouncing, as "a shallow and irreligious assumption," the cardinal principle of Protestantism, "that whatever God designs his creatures to believe or perform, he has plainly taught and declared." * A more learned and candid advocate of Episcopacy has said: "The claim of Episcopacy to be of divine institution, and therefore obligatory on the church, rests fundamentally on the one question — Has it the authority of Scripture? If it has not, it is not necessarily binding." †

The majestic simplicity of the New Testament, its revelation of pure and lofty truths, and its entire freedom from folly and fanaticism, stamp it with the impress of divinity, and attract the admiration of minds not yet prepared to acknowledge its heavenly origin. But, in passing from its pages to those of

---

* Marshall's Notes on the Episc. Pol. New York, 1844, p. 16. Of the accuracy with which this writer states facts, the reader may judge by the following statements: "The latest improvement upon the Baptist heresy is Mormonism." p. 345. "The great body of Methodists, following Dr. A. Clarke, have departed from the true doctrine of the Trinity." p. 346. These statements are made upon the highest "American authority." We may smile at the easy credulity of this "curate of Swallowcliffe;" but what shall we say of the Rt. Rev. Editor, Jonathan M. Wainwright, D.D., who endorses these and similar "old wives' fables?"

† Dr. Onderdonk's Episcopacy, tested by Scripture, p 1. Barnes' Reply, p. 99. See also Carson's refutation of Whately's illogical assumption with respect to the burden of proof, in his work on Baptism, ch. 1.

the early Christian fathers, we are conscious of an immense descent. The transition from Paul and John to Barnabas and Hermas, is felt as a departure from the teachings of inspired Apostles to the puerile conceits of a Judaizer and the drivelling of a dotard. It would be vain, if it were necessary, to attempt to supply the deficiences of the former by the latter. The hand of Providence has fixed a "great gulf" between the inspired and the uninspired Christian writings, and thus placed its condemnation upon those who are so "exceedingly zealous of the traditions" of the Fathers.

If the Scriptures were deficient or obscure, and the inquirer after truth were, therefore, driven to the Fathers, even that refuge would fail him. Their testimony is suspicious, partial, and contradictory; their works are corrupted and interpolated; and they themselves refer him back to the Scriptures as the only authoritative guide.*

To sustain the authority of the Fathers, and give plausibility to the scheme which rests the polity of

---

\* Goode's Divine Rule, chaps. 5–7. Daillé on the right use of the Fathers. Smyth's Pres. and Prel. pp. 314–328. Apostol. Succ. p. 79. Knapp's Theology, § 7. Dwight, 4, pp. 239–242. Neander's Church History, p. 407. Baumgarten Crusius, Compendium der Dogmengeschichte, Leipzig, 1840, § 20. Milton's Animadv. on Rem. Def. Sec. 4. Jortin says of Antiquity (or the Fathers), "she is like Briarius, and has a hundred hands, and these hands often clash and beat one another." Eccl. Hist. 2, p. 57.

the churches upon their testimony, it is sometimes affirmed that we are indebted to them for our knowledge and reception of the books which compose the sacred canon; and the inference thence derived, that if their testimony is valid in the one case, it is equally so in the other. But this is to confound things which are manifestly different. In settling the preliminary question, as to what books are canonical, we may refer to the testimony of the Fathers; but in order to ascertain what those books contain, we must consult the books themselves. The testimony of these early witnesses is to be calmly weighed, carefully scrutinized, and subjected to the rules which regulate our estimate of historical evidence. They are simply the media of proof, the means by which we arrive at a knowledge of the facts by which the question is to be decided. "The church of Jesus Christ, in the present day, does not believe in the divine authority of those books which it admits to be canonical, *because* the ancient church regarded them in the same light; but *because* there is satisfactory evidence that they were composed by men who wrote as they were moved by the Holy Ghost." *

* Arguments of Romanists Discussed and Refuted by Rev. Dr. Thornwell, p. 213. The testimony of the Fathers is the medium per quod, not the medium propter quod. Twesten's Vorlesungen, I. S. 433. Pictet Theol. Lib. 1. cap. IX. 4. Chillingworth, ch. 2. Answer, § 25.

The advocates of prelacy have not failed to charge upon other pedobaptists the inconsistency of admitting infant baptism upon the testimony of the Fathers, and rejecting the claims of episcopacy and the apostolical succession, although sustained upon the same foundation. From this dilemma Dr. Woods would extricate himself, by denying that it presents a fair statement of the case. "The chief historical argument in favor of infant Baptism does not," in his view, "arise from the fact, that the practice did at length generally prevail in the early ages; but from *the testimony* of the Fathers, that it was received from the apostles."\* But the historical argument here is extremely defective. Origen is the first of the Fathers who uses such language,† and he lived A. D. 185 — 254. His assertion, at so distant a remove from the time of the apostles, possesses little weight; especially as he ascribes to them, in the same connection, the doctrine that baptism cleanses from original sin.

I find no authority for this custom, either in the Scriptures, or the earliest Christian documents. If the baptism of infants be an ordinance of Christ, it must be plainly taught, by precept or example, in

---

\* Lectures on Church Government, p. 61.

† Ecclesia ab apostolis traditionem accepit etiam parvulis baptismum dare. Sciebant illi . . . quod essent in omnibus genuinæ sordes peccati, quae per aquam et spiritum ablu deberent. Orig. In ep. ad Rom. Opp. T. IV. p. 565.

the New Testament. If it be not so taught, to attempt to sustain it by an appeal to historical evidence, is to abandon the fundamental principle of Protestantism.

The period seems to be rapidly approaching when the Christian world must choose between the Scriptures and the traditions of men. If ever the man of sin is successfully assailed in his strong hold, it must be by the sword of the Spirit. The Bible is our only reliable armory. Equipped and supplied from this source, the man of God need not fear an encounter with the hosts of darkness. But if, rejecting the panoply which divine munificence has supplied, he resorts to earthly means of defence, he will fall in the struggle, oppressed with the mortifying consciousness that his unhallowed weapons have only precipitated his defeat. Like Milton's angels, he will be bruised and crushed beneath the weight of his own armor:

"Their armor helped their harm, crushed in and bruised
Into their substance pent, which wrought them pain
Implacable, and many a dolorous groan."
*Paradise Lost*, VI., 658.

## CHAPTER III.

### THE CHURCH OF CHRIST.

THE word Church (in the original Greek of the New Testament, ekklesia), means a congregation, or assembly; and the character of the assembly, to which it is applied, is to be ascertained by the use of the term in each particular instance. In its sacred use, it is confined to two meanings, referring either to a particular local society of Christians, or to the whole body of God's redeemed people.* Of the latter meaning of the word, the following are instances:

Christ loved the Church, and gave himself for it. Eph. 5 : 25. Gave him to be the head over all things to the Church, which is his body. Eph. 1 : 22, 23. The general assembly and Church of

---

* Campbell's Lectures on Eccl. History, Lec. 6, p. 100, 105, 106. King's Prim. Church, chap. 1. [It is sometimes asserted that Lord King subsequently renounced the views maintained in this book, Vid. Rose's note to Neander's Church History, Pref. p. 4. But the evidence is not satisfactory. Vid. Punchard on Congregationalism, p. 147.] Haldane's View of Social Worship, &c., ch. 5, § 1. Dagg's Essay on Communion, chap. 3, § 1. Dr. Johnson's **Gosp.** Developed, ch. 2. Barrow, Wks. (Am. Ed.) III. 312.

the first born, which are written in Heaven. Heb. 12 : 23.

It is this community of believers, the household of God, the whole family in heaven and earth, that constitutes the Holy Catholic Church, the kingdom of Christ in its internal development. It is one, and indivisible. Its members are known, certainly, only to Omniscience. Ordained unto eternal life before the foundation of the world, and in due time called, justified, sanctified, and glorified, they constitute the only real spiritual body of Christ, the fulness of Him that filleth all in all. Those who are members of this Church, and those alone, are interested in the benefits of the atonement, share the gifts of the Spirit, and enjoy the bliss which appertains to the communion of saints. Beyond its limits there is no salvation.*

The conception of the spiritual unity of the Church, which can be realized only by a living communion of all its members with the head, is clearly discerned in the instructions of Christ and his apostles, and is a glorious and precious truth. But it was soon misapprehended and perverted. The attempt was made to realize this unity in an

* The best definition of the Church of Christ, is that given by Augustine, and incorporated by Calvin in his Cat. Eccl. Genev. Quid est ecclesia? Corpus ac Societas fidelium quos deus ad vitam aeternam prædestinavit. See also Inst. IV. I. n. 2. 7. Pictet Theol. Art. XXVII. 7.

outward church, possessed of an external visible organization, and embracing, among its members, all the professors of Christianity in the world. The unity of the Spirit, which consists in faith and love, was merged in a unity of outward form.* The radical error of this theory consists in the assumption of an external visible union of Christians as the starting point from which to arrive at a real spiritual unity; whereas the reverse is the proper order of procedure. The primary and essential union of Christians consists in their connexion with a common head, and the possession of a common spirit; and particular societies of Christians can approximate to this unity, only in proportion as they realize in

---

\* Neander's Church Hist. p. 120. Münscher Dogmensge. [Ed. Von Cöln.] § 34. Meyer, § 25. The name, *holy Catholic Church*, first occurs in the epistle of the Church of Smyrna, concerning the martyrdom of Polycarp, written A. D. 169. Euseb. Hist. Eccl. IV. 15. The earliest patron of the notion was Irenaeus, († 201): it was fully developed by Cyprian, († 258,) in his book De unitate ecclesiae. Having referred to the history of Eusebius, I take this opportunity to caution the reader against trusting too implicitly to Cruse's translation of the work, published by Rev. R. Davis, Phila. It was made under Episcopalian influence, and is deeply tinged with it. Some of its errors have been noticed in Dr. Smyth's Confirmation Examined. Note A. p. 199. The expression *Catholic Church*, is also found in the larger collection of the epistles of Ignatius. Ep. ad Smyrn. c. 8 († 107). But the passage is not considered genuine. Münscher, § 34.

themselves the harmony and sympathy which distinguish the body of Christ.*

The minds of men had no sooner become possessed of this figment of a visible Catholic Church, than they saw the necessity of seeking for some visible head. This was indispensable to its completeness. Here we have the germ of the papa system, which has, at least, the merit of consistency; for the necessity of a visible head is a logical deduction from the doctrine of a visible Catholic Church. "Without a visible head," observes a distinguished Roman Catholic, "the whole view which the Catholic Church takes of herself, as a visible society representing the place of Christ, would have been lost, or rather would never have occurred to her. In a visible church, a visible head is necessarily included."†

The doctrine of a visible Catholic Church, although it seems to have been rejected by Luther, has been maintained by a large number of Protestants,‡ and even some of the advocates of Congre-

---

\* Marheineke Grundlehren der Christl. Dogmatik. S. 445. Nitzch. System der Christl. Lehre, § 188.

† Möhler's Symbolism, p. 377. Barrow, Unit. ch. VIII. 4.

‡ Hill's Divinity, p. 695. Dick's Theology, 2, p. 456. Smyth's Ecclesiastical Catechism, p. 11, with a copious citation of authorities. "The Church," says Ogilby, "is Christ's mystical body. This body of Christ is a *visible* body, made of many *visible* parts," Lectures on the Church, p. 13, New York, 1844.

gationalism have, with singular inconsistency, embraced the same view.* The subject demands, therefore, a thorough discussion. I am happy to say that Dr. Dagg, who has devoted much reflection to this topic, has, at my solicitation, furnished me with his views; and they are here inserted as a valuable and instructive addition to this work.

The question respecting the existence of a Visible Church Catholic, may be regarded, 1, as real, — 2, as verbal.

I. As *real*. The *real* question may be stated thus: Do all who profess the true religion constitute one organized society?

The following doctrine is maintained by Dr. Mason: There exists in the world a great society, composed of all who profess the true religion. This society is so organized that the parts are united in mutual dependence, and furnished with a principle of living efficiency in one common system, so as to bring the strength of the whole to operate on every part, or through all the parts collectively, as occasion may require. This society possesses the power of self-preservation, which includes, 1. A power of commanding the agency of any particular member; 2. A power of combining the agency of all her members; 3. A power of providing for her nourishment and health; 4. A power of expel-

* Walker's Church Discipline, p. 10, where he says the term Church, in Matt. 16 : 18, "appears to include, generally, such professed believers as hold the Christian faith and practice uncorrupted, throughout the world."

ling impurities and corruptions This society, with a regular succession of members, has existed visibly and publicly, from the days of Abraham to the present time.*

The following weighty objections lie against this doctrine:

1. It does not accord with the facts of history. All the professors of Christianity are not now so united, and it is certain that they have not been for ages past.

2. It favors the pretensions of the Roman Church. If any such society existed in the middle ages, its seat of power must have been at Rome.

3. The powers attributed to this society are inconsistent with the individual and personal responsibilities of its members. A power to command implies an obligation to obey. Now either the power must be exercised with infallible rectitude, or the members are bound to oppose it, and to obey God rather than men.

4. The Church organizations of primitive Christians did not extend beyond single congregations, which existed and acted independently of each other. Membership was voluntary, and no power was claimed to interfere in any wise with the individual and personal responsibility of any member. "To his own master he standeth or falleth."

5. The combination of individuals or of churches, for the purpose of exercising any controlling power whatever over the consciences of men, is the germ and spirit of Anti-Christ.

The doctrine to which these objections are opposed,

---

* Mason's Essays, pp. 5, 195, and elsewhere.

is a corruption of the Scripture doctrine, respecting what theological writers have called the Invisible Church. The saints in heaven, with all regenerate persons on earth, form a society which is called, in the language of inspiration, the Body of Christ, the Church of Christ, the People of Christ, the Flock of Christ, &c. Eph. 5 : 23–27 ; Matt. 1 : 21 ; 1 Peter 2 : 9 ; Luke 12 : 32 ; John 10 : 16 ; Heb. 12 : 23. The oneness of this body does not depend on any external organization, but arises from a spiritual union of all its members to Christ. It is compacted, not by any external force, nor by powers conferred on the members collectively, for the purpose of consolidation and control, but by that which every joint supplieth. Love is the cement of the parts, and the principle of living efficiency, growth and strength which pervades the whole. It maketh increase of itself in love. Membership in this society is, in the highest sense, voluntary, and all controlling power belongs, not to the body, but to the living head, Jesus Christ.

A few texts of Scripture, in which the term Church is used, have, by a mistaken interpretation of them, been supposed to favor the doctrine of a Visible Church Catholic. Dr. Mason refers to six as proof texts of this doctrine. It is a very remarkable circumstance that three of these six texts refer to a period in the history of Christianity, when no church of external organization existed, but that which was at Jerusalem. This was not a Catholic Church as distinguished from a particular Church ; and therefore these texts fail to prove anything in the question, except the difficulty of finding support for the doctrine in the word of God. The three passages are these: "The Lord added to the Church daily such as should be saved" Acts 2 : 47. " Saul made havoc of the church " — Acts 8 : 3. "I persecuted the Church of God" — 1 Cor. 15 : 9.

It is due, however, to the scheme of Dr. M., to say that it finds a Visible Church Catholic in existence at the period to which these texts refer: and it is due to the cause of truth to show that, in this very particular, the scheme involves incredible absurdity. He says, (pages 7 and 8,) "The Jews were not cut off till after the commencement and establishment of the new dispensation; that is, till after the Gentiles were taken in." According to this view of the subject, the excision of the Jews did not take place until after the conversion of Cornelius. Of consequence, the Jewish nation continued to be the Visible Church Catholic during the period to which the texts above quoted refer; and if they signify what they are cited to prove, their correct interpretation is as follows: "The Lord added to the Church;" i. e. to the Jewish nation. "Saul made havoc of the Church;" i. e. of the Jewish nation. "I persecuted the Church;" i. e. the Jewish nation. Comment is unnecessary.

Two causes have favored the misinterpretation of Scripture on this subject.

The first of these is an ambiguous use of the epithets visible and invisible. The saints in heaven are invisible to mortal eyes; but that part of the Church of the first born which still remains on earth, instead of being invisible, is a city set on a hill, that cannot be hid. The Saviour enjoined on his followers to let their light shine before men, that their good works, not their church organization, should be seen. The saints are distinguished from the ungodly world by their holiness of life; they need not a mark in their right hand or in their forehead, in order that their characters may be known and read of all men.

From the confounding of visibility with organization originated the remark of Dr. M.:* "Nor is it to be imagined that he (Saul) was able to pick out the elect and persecute them." The objects of persecution were not rendered visible to Saul by ecclesiastical organization. He did not pick them out by searching for their names in some church book. They are called "the disciples of the Lord"—the saints—and their relation to Christ is clearly intimated in the inquiry, "Why persecutest thou *me*?" The persecution was aimed at Jesus and his genuine disciples, and the guilt of it was estimated accordingly; nor was it necessary, in order that Saul should persecute the true disciples of Christ, that they should, on the one hand, be separated from any false professors who might chance to be among them; or, on the other hand, that they should be incorporated with these false professors, under some system of ecclesiastical government. Samson could burn the corn of the Philistines, without either separating the wheat from the tares or binding the whole in one great bundle. And a man may exclude the light of day from his chamber, though he neither "pick out" the sunbeams from the motes that float in

---

* This is the error of Bellarmine, de Ecclesia Mil. III. cap. 12. Non dici potest [ecclesia] societas hominum, nisi in externis et visibilibus signis consistat. See, also, Walter, Kirchenrecht, § 11.

them, nor press the light and the motes together into one consolidated mass. It should be remembered, however, that our present inquiry is not, whether the term *Church* includes, in its proper signification, false professors as well as true; but whether all professors, both true and false, constitute one organized society. So far, therefore, as the illustration of our present subject is concerned, it is of no importance whether the term *wheat* may properly signify the tares as well as the wheat; or the term *light*, the motes as well as the sunbeams. The only question is, whether one organized mass must be formed by the wheat and the tares, before they can be burned; or by the sunbeams and the motes, before they can be excluded.

Saul persecuted the Church when he persecuted such of its members as were within his reach. What was done to the part was regarded as done to the whole; and what was done against the members on earth was regarded as done against the head in heaven. On the same principle of interpretation we may understand the phrases: "Gaius, the host of the whole Church,"— Rom. 16: 23. "Give none offence to the Church of God,"— 1 Cor. 10: 32. They import hospitality to saints generally, and offence to saints generally. But that the saints should be entertained, offended, or persecuted, it is not necessary that they should be united in a Visible Church Catholic. These phrases are two of the remaining proof texts of Dr. M., and, like the three before quoted, prove nothing to his purpose.

A second cause which has contributed to the misinterpretation of Scripture on the subject, is a secularized view of the Christian ministry.

The Saviour, at Pilate's bar, declared, "My kingdom is not of this world. If my kingdom were of this world, then would my servants fight." In this declaration it is clearly implied, that the officers in his kingdom, like the kingdom itself, belong to another world. When he gave to Peter his great pastoral commission, in the memorable words, "Feed my sheep,— Feed my lambs,"— he prescribed spiritual duties, and appointed him a pastor, not to a single congregation, nor the Visible Church Catholic, but to the spiritual flock of Christ. The food administered is spiritual, and the recipients must be spiritual; the food is the sincere milk of the word. The recipients are the new-born babes who desire, and the believers, to whom Christ is precious. To suppose infant and adult members of the Visible Church Catholic to be intended, is a gross misconception of the Saviour's design.

When Peter met with Simon the Sorcerer, who had professed faith in Christ and been baptized, he did not on that account recognize him as one of Christ's sheep, and feed him accordingly; nor did he wait for the Church Catholic to bring its power to bear on this part of the great body, and expel the impurity. Peter regarded not his profession, but his spiritual state; not his relation to any visible Church, but his relation to Christ and things spiritual.

As Peter felt and acted, so felt and acted all the Apostles; and so they taught all the primitive ministers to feel and act. So Peter taught:

"The elders which are among you I exhort, who

am also an elder, and a witness of the sufferings of Christ, and also a partaker of the glory that shall be revealed :

"Feed the flock of God, which is among you, taking the oversight thereof; not by constraint, but willingly; not for filthy lucre, but of a ready mind;

"Neither as being lords over God's heritage, but being ensamples to the flock.

"And when the chief shepherd shall appear, ye shall receive a crown of glory that fadeth not away." 1 *Peter* 5 : 1 – 4.

So Paul taught the elders at Ephesus :

"Take heed, therefore, unto yourselves, and to all the flock over the which the Holy Ghost hath made you overseers, to feed the church of God, which he hath purchased with his own blood."— *Acts* 20 : 28.

So he taught his son Timothy :

"But if I tarry long, that thou mayest know how thou oughtest to behave thyself in the house of God, which is the church of the living God, the pillar and ground of the truth." — 1 *Tim.* 3 : 15.

These men referred every thing to eternity, and the heart-searching God. They regarded themselves as members of a spiritual body; and to their view the flock of God — the heritage of God — the house of God — the Church of God, consisted of those who were bound to them by spiritual ties, and whom they expected to meet in heaven.

The spirituality of the Christian ministry is vividly represented in 1 Cor. 12 chap. The body of Christ is one with many members, who are baptized into it by one Spirit, and drink of one Spirit. The eye, the ear, the hands, the feet, have their proper offices for the benefit of the whole. God hath set them in the body: and of none of them can it be said it is not of the body. All the diversities of gifts are from the same Spirit. From that member which sustains the highest and most important office, to that which occupies the least honorable place, one spiritual sympathy extends, which pervades the whole and excludes the possibility of schism. Assuredly this is not a description of the Visible Church Catholic. No false apostles, no false prophets, no ministers of Satan, in the form of ministers of righteousness, belong to this body. God has not set such in it. The Spirit has not baptized such into it. Such have not a care for the body. Of all such it may, with truth, be said, they are not of the body. Yet such officers and members must belong to the body, if Dr. M.'s interpretation of the 28th verse of this chapter is correct. This verse is his only remaining proof-text; and, like all the rest, utterly fails, when rightly interpreted, to serve the purpose for which it was quoted.

The evils resulting from secularized views of the Christian Church and ministry, are incalculable. This cause gave birth to the Man of Sin, and all the lordship which has been exercised over God's heritage. It has furnished, with sheep's clothing, the grievous wolves that have devoured the flock. To it may be ascribed, in chief part, the divisions which have been the opprobrium of Christianity and the stumbling-block of infidels. Having lost the unity of the spirit, the professors of religion, lest they should, by the independence of the churches, and the uncontrolled personal responsibility of every member, " be scattered abroad upon the face of the whole earth," resolved to build a tower, whose top should reach to heaven, and to inscribe on it the motto, VISIBLE UNITY. But, as it happened to the builders at Babel, their language became confounded, and their mad scheme ended in discord and division. Carnal leaders draw away disciples after them; and those who follow in such divisions are carnal. "While one saith, I am of Paul; and another, I am of Apollos; are ye not carnal, and walk as men?" Many schemes have been proposed, for the healing of these divisions, by the amalgamation of religious societies, but all will prove abortive, till men return to the unity of the Spirit.

Having examined the question concerning the Visible Church Catholic, as *real;* we proceed to consider it

II. As *verbal.* The verbal question may be thus stated: Is the term Church properly used to denote all the professors of the true religion taken collectively? This is a question of comparatively little importance; yet it deserves consideration, on account of the close connection which is often found to subsist between errors of thought and errors of language.

Men may be classified with respect to any property by which some are distinguished from others. The tall, the wise, the honest, the aged, are classes of which we may have occasion to think and speak. But these classes exist as classes in our minds only. The individuals of each class exist separately and independently, and may, in fact, have less to do with each other than with individuals of other classes. So, all the professors of the true religion may be classed together, and may be thought and spoken of as if forming a company distinct from the rest of mankind. It is therefore possible that the term Church may be used to denote this class of men, without implying that they are united in a visible organization. But can it be so used with propriety?

1. The term which is rendered Church in the New Testament, signifies an assembly. Dr. Mason says, "Whenever it occurs you are sure of an assembly, and nothing more." Now all the professors of religion, though they form a class in our mental conception, do not form an assembly. They never have assembled, and they never will assemble except on the day of judgment; and even then they will be separated from each other — some on the right hand, and some on the left.

2. In many of the examples in which the term Church is in the Scriptures used in its Catholic sense, it clearly denotes the body of real saints. Of those examples in which it has been supposed to denote all the professors of religion, not one has been found that, on a careful examination, requires this interpretation. To assign a new meaning, without necessity, is not in accordance with sound criticism.

3. It is not necessary to suppose that the inspired writers, whenever they employed the term Church in its Catholic sense, had present to their minds the distinction between true and false professors. A field of wheat may be called a field of wheat, without any regard to tares which may chance to be in it. So the several churches were addressed as believers, disciples, saints, &c., without regard to

false professors who might chance to be among them; yet the terms believers, disciples, and saints, do not acquire a new meaning from such application of them.

We may conclude, therefore, that the term Church, when used in its Catholic sense, denotes the body of real saints, as distinguished from all other persons; that it never denotes all the professors of religion, as distinguished from the body of real saints; and that it cannot include false professors of religion, unless it be in a vague and loose application of it.

It has been asked, Is not baptism the door into the Church? To this question it might be a sufficient reply, to refer to the tenth chapter of John, the only place of Scripture in which the door into the fold of Christ is mentioned. But if we must furnish an answer from the analogy of faith, rather than by direct appeal to Scripture, it will be needful to find the house, before we seek for the door. If there is no such building as the Visible Church Catholic, all inquiry about the door into it must, of course, be useless.

Baptism has been placed, by Christ, at the *beginning* of all the outward duties which he requires of his followers. It is, therefore, an *initiatory* service. But all agree that, as in the case of the Ethiopian Eunuch, baptism does not introduce to membership in a particular church; and it is clear that an individual must be a member of Christ's spiritual body, *before* baptism, or any other duty, can be acceptably performed. "Without me ye can do nothing."

For whose accommodation is this building needed,

of which baptism is the door? It denies shelter, of course, to all unbaptized persons; and all regenerate persons are better provided for, having been admitted into Christ's spiritual house. The only persons, therefore, who need it, are the unregenerate baptized, the followers of Simon the Sorcerer, who, while they profess Christ, are in the gall of bitterness and the bond of iniquity. Verily, for such persons, God's wise master builders are not required to provide a building; much less have they been authorized to place one of Christ's ordinances as the door into it. Pedobaptists have found difficulty in assigning a suitable apartment to their baptized infants; and have placed them, not so properly in the Church, as within its pale. Whether it would better accord with the analogy of this faith, to call baptism the gate, than the door, may be left for those to decide who are unwilling to keep the ordinances as they were delivered.

Baptism is not, like the Lord's supper, a social rite. It signifies the fellowship of the individual believer with Christ, not the fellowship of believers with one another. The obligation to be baptized is independent of the obligation to form social relations with other disciples, and is prior. Baptism is, therefore, a qualification for admission into a Church of external organization; but it does not confer membership.

# CHAPTER IV.

### PARTICULAR CHURCHES.

The Gospel is admirably adapted to man. Its disclosures of grace meet his wants, as a fallen, guilty creature; and its revelation of a future state satisfies the instinctive longings of his soul for immortality. The ecclesiastical polity of the New Testament is not less suited to him, as a social being. The instincts of our nature lead us to society, and many of our noblest qualities are called forth and nurtured by its influence. A particular Church is a society of believers baptized upon profession of their faith in Christ.

When the Apostles went forth, under the borad commission of their ascended Master, preaching the Gospel, they gathered together the fruits of their ministry, wherever they went, into local societies. These are the only Churches known to the New Testament. They constitute the external development of Christ's kingdom; and are employed, as nurseries, to prepare the genuine children of the kingdom for their ultimate and permanent abode.

A Church of Christ is a single congregation of professed believers, formed by the mutual agreement of its members, and designed for religious purposes. In this sense the word is used by the sacred writers more than sixty times. This is the view which has always been held by Baptists. "A particular gospel Church," says one of the earliest authorities in this country, "consists of a company of saints incorporated by a special covenant, into one distinct body, and meeting together in one place, for the enjoyment of fellowship with each other, and with Christ their head, in all his institutions, to their mutual edification, and the glory of God through the Spirit."* 2 Cor. 8: 5; Acts 2: 1.

Several important principles are involved in the scriptural definition of a gospel Church.

1. A Church is a single local society.
2. It is composed of professed believers.
3. It possesses the power of admitting to membership, exercising discipline, choosing its officers, and, in general, managing its own affairs.
4. It is independent of all other Churches.

Each of these points demands a separate investigation.

* Summary of Church Discipline of the Charleston Association, republished by Rev. D. Sheppard, Charleston, 1831. This Summary was prepared, probably, by Oliver Hart, Francis Pelot, and David Williams. Rippon's Register, for A. D. 1796, p. 511.

# CHAPTER V.

### A CHURCH IS A SINGLE LOCAL SOCIETY.

THIS is clear:

1. From the meaning and use of the term. We read in the New Testament of "the Church" in a particular city, village, and even house, and of "the Churches" of certain regions; but never of a Church involving a plurality of congregations.* "A bishoprick was but a single congregation."† There is no trace of any other kind of Church, presbyterian, diocesan, or national.‡

2. From the history of the Churches in the New Testament.

The Church at Jerusalem, the model after which the other Churches seem to have been formed,§ was a single congregation, which could meet together for social worship and the transaction of Church business.|| So also the Churches at Antioch, Co-

---

\* Acts 2: 47; 13: 1; Rom. 16: 1, 5; Col. 4: 15; Acts 9: 31; 15: 40, 41; 1 Cor. 16: 19.

† King's Prim. Church, cap. 2, § 12.

‡ R. Hall's Wks. 4, p. 394.

§ Gieseler's Church Hist. I. p. 56.

|| Acts 2: 44, 46; 4: 23—31; 5: 11—14. Comp. 3: 2, 11; 6: 1-6.

rinth, Ephesus, &c., were all single congregations.\*

It has been objected that the members of these Churches were too numerous to constitute a single congregation.† But if the New Testament alludes, in these cases, to only one Church, and affirms that "the whole Church" did meet together and transact business in common, the objection is negatived by the authority of Scripture. The argument which attempts to disprove the congregational polity of the Church at Jerusalem, is similar to that by which the baptism of its members has been assailed. The narrative in Acts plainly intimates that the three thousand converts were baptized, (or immersed.) But it is objected that they were too numerous to be baptized, and therefore must have been sprinkled. In either case the baptized congregationalist rejects the unwarrantable assumption.‡

---

\* Acts 13: 1-4; 14: 25—27; 15: 22—30; 1 Cor. 11: 20, 33; 14: 23, 26.

† Dick's Theol. 2, p. 478. Hill, p 692. Milner, Church Hist. Cent. 3, ch. 20.

‡ The baptism of the three thousand is not so improbable a case after all. I baptized, on one occasion, seventy-six persons in seventeen minutes, and that without any special view to expedition. I did not even know that any one was noticing the time. The twelve apostles, baptizing at the same rate, would have baptized the three thousand in fifty-five minutes and fifty-five seconds!

Since writing the above, I have learned that "Elder

## CHURCH POLITY.

It is not, however, material to the argument to prove that the members of a Church actually did meet together for social worship. The Scriptures inform us that this was the case at Jerusalem. In other cities, where the number of members was very large, local convenience may have been consulted; and there may have been portions of the Church that held their religious meetings in different places, but still constituting, as in some of our large cities, branches or arms of the Church located in those cities. This is rendered probable, by the existence of a plurality of bishops. It is sufficient to show that the Churches of the New Testament were single societies, that the members of a certain locality constituted a Church, not Churches, and that they were addressed by the Apostles, as a unit and not a plurality. Even if it be conceded, therefore, that the number of elders, found in the primitive Churches, was rendered necessary by their habit of assembling in different places of worship, this does not affect the congregational character of these Churches; since each body of elders was addressed

---

Courtney baptized seventy-five persons in the basin on the canal, in Richmond, Va. He had assistants, who led the candidates to and from him; and he performed the whole in seventeen minutes, notwithstanding he was seventy years old." Life of John Leland, Richmond, 1836, p. 33. For similar cases among the earlier Christians, see Christian Rev. III. p. 91.

as the officers of "the Church," plainly evincing that the community to which they were attached, constituted a single society.

3. From the large number of distinct Churches which are mentioned in the New Testament.

Churches seem to have been instituted upon the principle of local convenience. Whenever a body of converts were found, who could conveniently assemble together for the discharge of the duties of Church members, there a Church was organized. Hence we find separate Churches contiguous to each other. The Church at Cenchrea was only nine miles from that at Corinth.* In the epistle to the Colossians the names of four distinct Churches occur, located within a distance of five miles.† Five and thirty different Churches are referred to in the New Testament, besides a great many more that are comprehended in the general designation, "Churches of Asia," "Churches of Macedonia," &c.‡

This view of a Christian Church is so obviously scriptural, as to have commanded the assent of a large number of historians and theologians. The

---

\* Rom. 16: 1.

† Col. 4: 13—16. Calmet states that Hierapolis and Laodicea were five miles apart, and Colosse midway between them.

‡ Punchard, on Congregationalism, p. 49, gives a list of the thirty-five churches. Also, Dr. Curtis, Bible Episcopacy, p. 97.

following are a few of many authorities that might be cited:

"The simplest conception of a Church is that of a community of believers, dwelling in the same place, and associated for the promotion of Christ's kingdom." Schleiermacher. Kurtze Darstellung des theol. Stud. § 277.

In the primitive age "a Church and a diocese seem to have been, for a considerable time, co-extensive and identical. And each Church or diocese, and consequently each superintendent [i. e. bishop or elder], though connected with the rest by the ties of faith and love and charity, seems to have been perfectly independent, as far as regards any power of control." Archbishop Whately, Kingdom of Christ, p. 136.

"A Church I take to be a voluntary society of men, joining themselves together of their own accord, in order to the public worshipping of God, in such manner as they judge acceptable to him, and effectual to the salvation of their souls." Locke, Letter I. on Toleration. Wks. fol. 2, p. 235.

"In no approved writers, for the space of two hundred years after Christ, is there any mention made of any other organical, visibly professing Church, but that only which is parochial, or congregational." J. Owen, Wks. 20, p. 132.*

---

* Haldane, Social Worship, chap. 5, § 1. Leonard Bacon, Manual for Church Members, p. 15.

# CHAPTER VI.

### MEMBERS OF A CHURCH.

THE primary and indispensable qualification for membership in a particular Church, consists in a connection with the general Church, or body of Christ. "Every one is so far a member of Christ's Church as he is a member of Christ's body."* Each particular Church seeks to represent, in itself, the kingdom of Christ, and ought, therefore, to be composed entirely of spiritual materials. It is no part of its design to embrace unbelievers, and prepare them for the kingdom of heaven. They have no right to its privileges and blessings. They are intruders at its ordinances. No ecclesiastical recognition of them as children, can change their relation as aliens and strangers; and they who introduce them contravene the declared will of the great Head of the Church. The gates of his kingdom are open to none but converted men. It is, therefore, the imperative duty of the Churches to admit to membership none but such as give satisfactory evidence that they have been born again. This was the practice of the apostles.†

---

\* T. Jackson on the Church, p. 19. Phila., 1844.

† "No one," says Marheinecke, "is a member of the Church by birth: he becomes one first by the new birth." Die Grundlehren der christlichen Dogmatik. § 693.

That the Churches planted by them were composed of such as they deemed real believers is evident,

1. From the addresses of the different epistles:—"Paul, to all that be in Rome, beloved of God, called saints. To the Church of God at Corinth, to them that are sanctified in Christ Jesus, called saints. To the saints which are at Ephesus and the faithful in Christ Jesus. To the saints in Christ Jesus, which are at Philippi. Peter, to them that have obtained like precious faith."

2. From the general tenor of the epistles. In proof of this position, it is simply necessary to refer the reader to these inspired compositions themselves. Every allusion to the origin of the Churches; every description of the character of the members; every exhortation, rebuke, and warning; all directions with respect to their government and discipline, bear ample evidence that they were contemplated by the authors of the epistles, as comprising only those who had made a credible profession of their faith in the Redeemer. Had the apostles sanctioned the admission of unconverted men into the Churches, their practice would have been at variance with the spirit of their subsequent communications to them. To address such persons as the children of light and the temples of the Holy Ghost, would have been to use language without meaning, or singularly delusive. The limits of this work forbid an extended

investigation of this topic. The reader is requested to consult the following passages of Scripture, in which the character of Church members is clearly exhibited :* Col. 3 : 9 ; 1 Thess. 5 : 5 ; 1 Cor. 6 : 19 ; 5 : 7 ; 3 : 9—17 ; 2 Cor. 7 : 8, 18 ; 6 : 14, 18 ; Acts 8 : 26—40 ; 1 Pet. 2 : 5.†

3. The design of Christian Churches affords additional evidence that none but believers were contemplated in their organization. This part of the subject has been presented in so just and beautiful a view by a pious pedobaptist writer, that I cannot do better than to transcribe his words :— " The Church is a sacred enclosure taken in from the world — brought into cultivation by the Divine Husbandman,

---

* In the famous controversy between Pres. Edwards, and Solomon Williams, concerning the half-way covenant, the former took the broad scriptural ground, that none but such as gave credible evidence of their faith in Christ should be admitted to the Lord's Supper. But, as a pedobaptist, he was obliged to admit that those who had been baptized in infancy were "in some sort members of the Church." In this they were both agreed. Here Williams erected his strong battery, and managed it with great effect. He proved that the position of his opponent, if maintained, would annihilate infant baptism. Either that ordinance must be given up, or Edwards must surrender. He did not choose to abandon infant baptism, and was vanquished, not by the truth of his opponent, but by his own error. Edwards, Humble Inquiry, Works 4, p. 423—428. Curtis, Bib. Episc. p. 173.

† Haldane, Social Worship, ch. 6. Punchard Congregationalism, pp. 40—47.

and intended to be filled exclusively with the plants of righteousness. He designed the Church to be his own *peculium* : it is the only fortress which he holds in a revolted world ; and he intended, therefore, that no authority should be known in it, no laws acknowledged, but his own ; that no parties should obtain admission, but those ' who are called, and chosen, and faithful ; ' so that to open its gates for the entrance of any of the revolted, however specious the pretext, is a betrayal of the most sacred trust, and treachery to the great cause of Christ." Harris, Great Teacher, p. 214.

So writes Dr. Smyth, and, indeed, every evangelical writer, when not thinking of infant baptism. " Only those who make a credible profession of their faith in Christ, can be admitted as members of the Church of Christ ; because its privileges, by their very nature, are intended only for those who, in the judgment of charity, are disciples of Christ."[*]

If these views are just and scriptural, it is evident that no place is provided, in a Christian Church, for such as do not, or cannot profess their faith in Christ. As infants belong to this class, they are excluded by the original and divine constitution of a

---

[*] Eccl. Catechism, p. 80. This is excellent. But we find, in the same work, among the meanings ascribed to the word Church, the following : "The whole body of those, *with their children*, who profess the true religion." p. 10, Dick Theol. 2, p. 380, 460. Punchard, p. 40.

Christian Church. Upon the same principle they are excluded from baptism, since the ordinance is the appointed method of professing our faith in the Redeemer. The grounds upon which the right of infants to baptism is based, are various and contradictory; they are all alike unscriptural. "It is a common sentiment," observes one of its advocates, "that the baptism of children makes them members of the Church; but this is an error. Their baptism does not make them members, it only recognizes their right of membership already existing; their membership is not founded upon their baptism, but their baptism upon their membership."* But another affirms † that "the children of the members cannot be considered as members of the Church, being incapable of fulfilling the duties of that relation." A more recent writer teaches that baptism "brings the child into the Church of God, to which he has promised his favor and blessings—translates it from the kingdom of darkness into the visible kingdom of God's dear Son, on earth." ‡ There is plainly a schism on this point among pedobaptists,

---

\* Rev. S. Helfenstein. The Church of God. Am. Bib. Repos. 2, p. 314. C. C. Jones, Catechism, p. 246.

† Haldane, Social Worship, p. 321. He afterwards renounced infant baptism. Indeed it is surprising, that one who could write such a book should practice it.

‡ Rev. W. Hodges, Infant Baptism tested by Scripture and History, Phil. 1844, p. 243.

according to the views of the respective denominations to which they belong. The Papal and Episcopal Churches maintain that the infant is made a member of the Church by baptism; while the Lutheran and Presbyterian Churches contend that it is entitled to the ordinance, because it is already a member.* To the former class the Methodist Episcopal Church seems to belong. Mr. Wesley says: "By baptism we are admitted into the Church, and, consequently, made members of Christ, its Head."† Dr. Bond has taken a different view. "Baptism is not properly the *initiating* ordinance, by which we become subjects of this kingdom, [Messiah's] but the ratifying or sealing ordinance, by which we are so acknowledged by the Church and ministry of Christ. Children are initiated into the kingdom at their birth."‡ This, it will be perceived, throws the door open to all children. But pedobaptists have usually restricted the ordinance to the offspring of believers. Even upon this point, however, there

---

\* C. G. Neudecker. Lehrbuch der christl. Dogmengesch. § 56, where he says that the "Lutheran, Reformed, Roman and Grecian Catholic Churches supported infant baptism against the fanatical Anabaptists and Mennonites, and against Schwenkfield on the ground that it was, in general, necessary to salvation." Hinton's Hist. Baptism, p. 338.

† Preservatives, p. 146—150, quoted by Booth. Vindic. Bap. Sec. 1.

‡ N. Y. Christian Advocate, copied in Biblical Recorder. N. C., Jan. 27, 1844.

is another schism.* It is refreshing to turn from the conflicting opinions of men to the simple word of God, which contains no intimation of infant membership, either before or after baptism, and recognizes only baptized believers as the constituents of a gospel Church.

The abettors of infant baptism have, usually, rested its claims upon an alledged identity of the covenant of circumcision and the covenant of grace; and, assuming that baptism has taken the place of circumcision, have argued that, as children were formerly admitted to the latter ordinance, they ought now to be to the former. To examine at length all the arguments by which this subject has been mystified, does not comport with the limits of this little book. It will be sufficient, however, to expose some of the leading assumptions involved in the theory in question.

---

* Archbishop Leighton writes to one of his friends: "Touching baptism, freely my thought is, it is a weak notion, taken up on trust almost generally, to consider so much, or at all, the qualifications of the parents. Either it is a benefit to infants, or it is not. If none, why then administered at all? But if it be, then why should the poor innocents be prejudged of it for the parents' cause?" Works, p. 681. Baptism, in his view, "signifies and seals our washing from sin and our new birth in Jesus Christ," p. 506. The seal, however, proves to be very brittle, for "the open wickedness of the most testifies against them, that though sprinkled with water in baptism, yet they are strangers to the power and gracious efficacy of it; they are swearers, cursers, drunkards, unclean," p. 223.

1. It involves the assumption, that the covenant of circumcision is the covenant of grace. If this were the case, all who lived before Abraham, as well as all, who, in subsequent times, are not in the line of circumcision, would be excluded from the covenant of grace. What, then, becomes of Abel and other antediluvian patriarchs? The truth is, that circumcision stands in no necessary relation to spiritual blessings. It is the distinguishing mark of a race, the members of which are determined by natural descent. The possession of spiritual blessings by the circumcised is not invariable, but accidental to the rite; and is determined upon other principles. Its design was, together with other rites and ceremonies, which were peculiar to the Jewish people, to segregate, and, consequently, preserve the nation. "These peculiarities," observes the learned historian of the Hebrew Commonwealth, "formed the foundation upon which was built the great partition wall between them and other nations."*

2. It assumes that the covenant made with Abraham, which involved spiritual blessings, and the covenant of circumcision are identical. But it is evident, from the third chapter of Galatians, that these covenants are distinct. The former was made,

* Jahn. Heb. Com. p. 38, 138. So Photius and Chrysostom and Theodoret, quoted by Dr. Brantly, Baptist Library, 3, p. 400.

according to the statement of the apostle, four hundred and thirty years before the delivery of the Law. This computation makes it coeval with the calling of Abraham out of Ur of the Chaldees, an event which occurred twenty-four years before the covenant of circumcision.

3. It confounds the natural with the spiritual seed of Abraham; the children of the flesh with the children of the promise. These are clearly distinguished in the word of God.* The argument on this point is simple and direct. The passages which are cited in support of infant baptism, in connection with the Abrahamic covenant, must refer either to his natural, or his spiritual seed. If to the former, Gentile infants are excluded, since they are not the lineal descendants of the patriarch; if to the latter, all infants are excluded by the very terms which designate the relation. "Know ye therefore that they which are of faith, the same are the children of Abraham."

The above remarks are sufficient to expose the flimsy foundation upon which this theory is built; the weakness of which is so apparent, that it has been abandoned by many pedobaptists themselves.†

The recognition of unconverted persons, as members of a Christian Church, is an evil of no ordinary

---

\* Gal. 3 : 18, 29; 4 : 28, cf. Rom. 9 : 7, 9.

† Stuart on the O. T. p. 394. Letters of David (Jones) and Job (Dagg) on the Lectures of Dr. Woods, Lec. 3. Carso on Baptism, p. 214, 237. Hinton, ch. 5, § 1.

magnitude. It throws down the wall of partition which Christ himself has erected, and obliterates the distinction between the Church and the world. A society composed of believers, and sustained and extended by spiritual instrumentalities, has the promise of the Redeemer pledged for its perpetuation. Such a community is indestructible. The body,

> "Vital in every part,
> Cannot, but by annihilating, die."

It becomes the disciples of the Saviour to guard well the door of admission into their fraternity. Upon their fidelity, in this respect, depend its efficiency, prosperity, and safety. An accession of nominal Christians may enlarge its numbers, but cannot augment its real strength. A Church that welcomes to the privileges of Christ's house, the unconverted, under the specious pretext of increasing the number of his followers, in reality betrays the citadel to his foes. They may glory in the multitudes that flock to their expanded gates, and exult in their brightening prospects; but the joy and the triumph will be alike transient. They have mistaken a device of the enemy for the work of God. They hailed, as they thought, an angel of light; they have received Satan. I admire and love the many sincere and zealous Christians that are found in such Churches; but I fear that this Trojan horse will finally prove their ruin.

On the subject of infant baptism, and what seem to me to be its legitimate tendencies, I have recorded my sentiments without reserve, and, I trust, without offence. I impeach no man's motives; nor do I question the piety and sincerity of those of my Christian brethren who believe that this practice is sanctioned by the divine command. Many pedobaptists are among the lights and ornaments of the age; their ministry has been blessed of God to the extension of the Redeemer's kingdom, and their Churches present numerous examples of pure and unaffected piety. Such men would not, knowingly, contravene the law of Christ. They would welcome the obloquy of the world, and even the agonies of martyrdom, in obedience to the command of their Lord and King, and rejoice that they were counted worthy to suffer for Christ's sake. It is impossible not to admire and love men whose faith and practice associate them with Baxter, Leighton, Edwards, and Martyn, and who breathe their heavenly spirit. While I think I see and regret their errors, I would extend to them the same indulgence which I ask for my own.

## CHAPTER VII.

### RIGHTS OF A CHURCH.

As it was manifestly the design of the Redeemer that his Churches should embrace only such as professed his name, and submitted to his will as the law of their life, so, also, he has entrusted to them the high privileges of self-government under Him. The New Testament, which contains the charter, constitution, and discipline of these voluntary societies of Christians, defines and limits their rights. Whatever powers have been expressly delegated to them, they may exercise: the assumption of others is an unauthorized usurpation. The Churches are bound to retain the full possession of the rights and privileges committed to them by Christ. They have as little authority to diminish, as to increase them. Acquiescing in the wisdom of the divine plan, and grateful for the advantages it secures, they should firmly resist every invasion of its supremacy, or violation of its spirit.

The divine constitution of the Churches is equally illustrative of the wisdom and the condescension of the Redeemer. In committing the government of his chosen people to themselves, he has graciously evinced his confidence in their fidelity and love. And this confidence has not, usually, been betrayed. The enormous evils which, under the guise of Christianity, have cursed the Church and the world, were the legitimate fruits of priestcraft, prelacy, and hierarchal domination. The great body of the people, when left to themselves, have always retained their loyalty and love to their invisible king.

1. Every Christian Church possesses the right of discipline, formative and corrective. With its divine constitution in its hands, defining the qualifications which entitle to membership, it is its province to determine as to the possession of those qualifications, in the case of every applicant. Its nature as a voluntary society, involves the right to admit and to exclude. Primitive Christians constituted a voluntary compact; they gave themselves first to the Lord, and then to one another; and were always addressed as those who had decided for themselves on the solemn subject of adherence to Christ.

The fundamental principles of Church discipline are laid down in Matt. 18 : 15 : 18. Here the Saviour enjoins the course to be pursued towards an offending brother, and designates "*the Church*" as the tribunal of ultimate appeal. What, then, is the Church? The context affords a satisfactory reply. "Where two or three are gathered together in my name, there am I." This is the Church to which

Christ alludes. It is gathered in his name, and blessed with his presence; and is, therefore, competent to decide a question involving the interests of his cause. The Scriptures recognize no higher authority. It is worthy of remark that in the organization of this ecclesiastical court for the trial of offences, the officers of the Church are not even mentioned. Their presence is not considered indispensable. "No officer is here. It is not the Church clerk, nor the parties that have neglected to summon him. The Church's Head, the Lord Jesus Christ, has left him out." \*

To evade the force of these remarks, and take from the people the discipline of the Church, it is contended that the word, in this place, refers to the officers or representatives of the Church.† But, surely, nothing but the most imperative critical necessity would justify such an unusual interpretation: an interpretation which, so far from being demanded by the exigency of the case, is positively excluded. Some of the best critics, even among Episcopalians, sustain this, the natural and usual explanation of the passage.‡ The correctness of this interpretation

---

\* Curtis, Bib. Episc. p. 145.

† Smyth, Eccl. Catech. 1, § 1, 6. Dr. Miller, Presbyterianism, p. 58.

‡ "The Church or particular community of which he is a member." Bland, Bloomfield. The old English versions of 1539 and 1541 render: "Tell it to the congregation."

is supported by the directions which were subsequently given to the Churches by the apostles. Rom. 16 : 17 ; I Cor. 5 : 9—13 ; II Thess. 3 : 6, 14, 15. If the reader will turn to those passages of Scripture, he will see that they recognize the right of the Churches to discipline offenders, and demand its exercise.

If any thing further were necessary to vindicate the rights of God's people, and sustain them against the assumptions of clerical supremacy, it would seem that the case of the Corinthian Church is unambiguous and decisive. On an occasion which demanded the most stringent application of corrective discipline, even an apostle does not venture to trench upon the prerogatives of the brotherhood. He does not interfere, in virtue of his apostolic authority, to coerce them ; he does not address their officers ; but takes occasion, in an epistle "to the Church of God which is at Corinth," to suggest a proper method of procedure. 'In the name of our Lord Jesus Christ, when ye are gathered together and my spirit, with the power of the Lord Jesus Christ, to deliver such an one unto Satan [i. e. to cast him out of the Church and send him back to the world, which is the kingdom of Satan.] Purge out, therefore, the old leaven." I Cor. 5 : 4—7, 13. The faithful exercise of discipline in this case, seems to have been blessed by God to the restoration of the Church's purity and peace. The incestuous person was led to repentance. The apostle again tenders the brethren his advice. "Sufficient to such a man is this *punishment, which was inflicted* of many, [that is excommunication by the majority of the Church] so that ye ought, rather, to forgive him and comfort him. Wherefore I *beseech* you that ye would confirm your love to him." II Cor. 2 : 6—11. "The apostle does not here," observes Punchard, "speak as one having alone the key of the Corinthian Church; but contrariwise, as one who recognized the power 'of the many' to act in the matter. He does not *command* the Church to restore the penitent, but he '*beseeches*' them : much less does he restore the excommunicated person by the authority vested in himself as a minister of the gospel of Christ." \* The tone of rebuke with which the apostle addressed the Church, not its officers, shows that the responsibility rested with them, and that they were chargeable with gross dereliction of duty. Had this not been the case, his censure would have been equally unjust and unkind.†

The Christian system involves a provision of mercy for the human race, irrespective of natural distinctions. It is the divinely appointed remedy

---

\* Congregationalism, p. 65. Haldane, p. 346.

† Coleman, Prim. Ch., ch. 5, p. 90. Bacon, Manual, p. 22. Walker, Church Discipline, § 10. King, ch. 7, § 3.

for guilt and depravity; and as these are the universal characteristics of our fallen race, it proffers its redeeming and sanctifying grace to woman as well as to man. But it is no part of its design to disturb the natural relation of the sexes, or obliterate the distinctions which the Creator has himself appointed. Hence, in the organization of the Church it has pleased divine wisdom to sanction and perpetuate the subordination of woman to man, by excluding her from any share in the administration of its government. To woman was assigned the distinguishing honor of giving birth to the Saviour of mankind; and this fact alone is sufficient to redeem Christianity from the imputation of depreciating or slighting the sex, even though it confers upon her no other prerogatives in the church than silence, obedience, and the personal illustration of the graces appropriate to her high vocation. "Let the woman learn in silence with all subjection. But I suffer not a woman to teach, nor to usurp authority over the man, but to be in silence."—1 Tim2: 11–12. This passage, compared with 1 Cor. 14 : 34, amounts to a total exclusion of the sex from the public instruction and government of the Church.* It has been supposed that 1 Cor. 11 : 5, conflicts with the other passage of the epistle to which I have referred. "We must account for this

---

* Vid. Macknight and Bloomfield, in loc.

apparent contradiction," says Neander, "by supposing that Paul, in the second passage, (1 Cor. 11: 5,) cited an instance of what occurred in the Corinthian Church, and reserved his censures for another place.\* For Mr. Mercer's views, which accord with my own, with respect to the participation of females in the government of the Church, see his Memoirs by Rev. C. D. Mallary, App. p. 447. The Discipline of the Charleston Association, p. 132, declares that "female members are excluded from all share of rule or government in the Church." Some of our Churches practise otherwise. Mr. Punchard says: "It is generally thought desirable that the female members of a Church should be present at the transaction of all ordinary business, for their satisfaction and instruction; but it is utterly inconsistent with established usage, for females to take any part in business transactions."—p. 170.† This unscriptural custom

---

\* Planting of the Church, p. 38. We have an example of the same method of teaching in ch. 8. T. Grantham thus explains the passage, "Every woman praying or prophesying," &c. He says: "The whole Church is said to do a thing, when it is actually performed by one person or a few," cf. ch. 14 : 23, 24. Hence a woman is said to pray, when she does so through the person who prays in the Church. Christianismus Primitivus, Part II. B. III. c. 7, § 2—London, 1678.

† Benedict, History Baptist, 2, p. 472. "There were some fanatical sects in the ancient Church, such as the

originated, probably, in that spurious delicacy which induces some ministers, on baptismal occasions, to administer the ordinance to the women first, a species of refinement which partakes more of modern chivalry than primitive Christianity. Women who appreciate their true position will decline the honor.

2. A Church possesses the right to choose its own officers.

The evidence of the Scriptures in support of this position is clear and conclusive. They record instances of the election of an apostle, and of deacons, delegates, and elders, each by a popular vote. It need excite no surprise that the position has been vigorously assailed.* The importance of the principle at stake, justifies both the attack and the defence. If the clergy have been invested with the sole power of appointment, they are right in contending for it. If, on the contrary, the Head of the Church has deposited this prerogative with those whose interests are most intimately involved in its exercise, it becomes them to resist clerical encroachment, with the vigilance and firmness of Christ's freemen.

The first instance on record is the appointment

---

Montanists and Collyridians, who authorized and encouraged women to speak, dispute, and teach in public. But the sentiment of the Church has uniformly been opposed to such indecencies." Coleman, Christ. Antiq. p. 118.

* Taylor, Spir. Desp. p. 324–333.

of an apostle.—Acts 1 : 15–26. If the apostles had considered themselves authorized, in any case, to act upon their own responsibility, it would have been on this occasion, when a vacancy was to be supplied in their own body. But we hear nothing of the apostolic power of appointment. They settle at the outset the principle which is to determine such matters, by committing the choice of an apostle, under God, to the people. The Church at Jerusalem was vested with the appointing power. Even if this extraordinary case were an exception, it would not negative the evidence in favor of popular suffrage, which is derived from other instances. These will now be examined.

In Acts 6 : 1–6, the election of deacons occurs. The apostles call together "the multitude of the disciples," and propose the matter to them. The " whole multitude" unite in the choice of the seven, and " set them before the apostles for prayer and the imposition of hands." No satisfactory explanation of this case can be given, but that which supposes that in the judgment of the apostles it was the prerogative of the Church to choose its own officers.* The comment of a distinguished Episcopalian on this transaction is worthy of notice. "The apostles, the heads of the Church, prescribed the qualifications for the office, the people chose the persons

---

\* Punchard, p. 59. Coleman, p. 56.

who were thus worthy, and the apostles ordained them to the appointed office. Every Church, we infer therefore, is entitled and bound to follow this plan of conduct . . . . . The same rules which were on the present occasion prescribed, we have reason to suppose, were observed likewise in the nomination of bishop and deacons in the Churches."* Although he denies that any "possible authority can be derived from this portion of Scripture to sanction the laity in taking upon themselves the choice and appointment of their respective ministry," he makes every concession for which Congregationalists have usually contended. They insist upon the right of the laity to elect their own officers, but admit that the act of a presbytery is necessary to induct them regularly into office.†

The position which I have taken is confirmed by the fact that even in the appointment of individuals to less important duties than those which appertain to official station in the Church, the apostles invited the counsel and coöperation of the brethren, and submitted to their choice. Acts 15 : 22–29, (comp. II. Cor. 8 : 19,) records an instance of the election of delegates. "Then pleased it the apostles and elders with the whole Church, [at Jerusalem] to

---

\* Townsend, N. T. Part 9, note 30.

† Punchard, p. 164. Church Discip. Charleston Assoc- ch. 2. Haldane, ch. 7.

send chosen men [having chosen men from among themselves to send them*] of their own company to Antioch." The letter which they bore was addressed in the name of "the apostles and elders and brethren," evincing the participation of the Church in the Mission to Antioch.† On this point Neander remarks: "It is evident that the first deacons, and the delegates who were authorized by the Church to accompany the apostles, were chosen by the Churches themselves. From these examples we may infer that a similar method was adopted in the appointment of elders."‡

The instances cited above are amply sufficient to determine in whose hands is deposited the right to appoint to office in a gospel Church. They are clear and explicit. The proof derived from them cannot, therefore, be invalidated by the citation of those equivocal cases upon which the abettors of prelacy have expended so much of their strength. No rule of interpretation is more indisputable, than that obscure portions of Scripture are to be explained by those which are perspicuous. These remarks are applicable to the transaction referred to in Acts

\* Bloomfield.
† Potter cuts the knot here, by rejecting "*and*" from the the text, and reading "the apostles and elders, brethren." The design of this artifice is obvious. Church Government p. 291. London, 1839.
‡ Pflantz und Leit. der ch. Kirche. S, 703.

14 : 23, 24. "And when they, (Paul and Barnabas) had *ordained* them elders in every Church," &c. Attempts have been made to sustain the doctrine of popular rights, by showing that it is implied in the meaning of the term *ordained*. Beza went so far as to render the passage " when they had created elders by suffrage;"\* for which he has been severely censured by Campbell.† Many modern writers have followed Beza's example.‡ A recent advocate of episcopacy contends that the word does not necessarily imply a popular election.§ In this I am compelled, on critical grounds, to concur. The term, (which is composed of two words signifying *to lift up the hand,*) did originally signify to choose by suffrage, in accordance with the custom of the Greeks; but it acquired, in common use, a secondary signification, and was employed to express an appointment in any way. It is manifestly so employed by Josephus.‖ It does not appear, therefore, that any proof can be derived from this instance in favor of a popular election. With as little reason can it be employed on the other side. In a succinct history, like Luke's, it is not to be expected that he should enter into the details of every trans-

---

\* Quumque ipsi per suffragia creâssent presbyteros.
† Gospels. Diss. 10 Part. 4, 7.
‡ Coleman, p. 51. Punchard, p. 59.
§ Chapin, Primitive Church, p. 155, New Haven, 1846.
‖ Antiq. 1, 13, 2, 2.

action which he records. It is sufficient that he has furnished us with indubitable instances of election to office by the suffrages of the brethren. All other cases must be settled in conformity with the principle there laid down or exemplified, so that wherever he informs us that the apostles ordained elders, it is to be understood that it was with the consent and concurrence of the people.*

On this point it has been well remarked by Haldane: "That the pastoral relation between teachers or pastors and a church can only be formed by mutual consent, is not only manifest from the conduct of the Apostles recorded in the Scriptures, but is necessarily implied in the nature of this relation, considered in every view. It is not less absurd to maintain, that because we have no direct example of a church choosing its own elders, that this matter is left undetermined, than it would be to argue, that since the word of God has not declared the marriage union is to be entered into by mutual choice, it is doubtful whether this be required. Such obvious principles as necessarily result from our nature and

---

* "When Paul gives Titus power to appoint rulers of the Church," says Neander, "who had the requisite qualities, nothing is thereby determined as to the nature of the election; it does not necessarily follow that an election by the Church itself is absolutely excluded." Church Hist., p. 108, Augusti. in Coleman. Antiq. p. 131. Neander, in Coleman's Prim. Ch. Introduction, p. 10.

circumstances, are frequently taken for granted in Scripture." *

The evidence in support of this position is so clear and full that it is admitted by the highest authorities in ecclesiastical history.

"In those primitive times each Christian Church was composed of the *people*, the *presiding officers*, and the *assistants* or *deacons*. . . The highest authority was in the *people*, or the whole body of Christians. . . The assembled people, therefore, elected their own rulers and teachers, or by their authoritative consent, received them, when nominated to them. They also, by their suffrages, rejected or confirmed the laws that were proposed by their rulers, in their assemblies; they excluded profligate and lapsed brethren, and restored them; they decided the controversies and disputes that arose; they heard and determined the causes of presbyters and deacons; in a word, the people did everything, that is proper for those in whom the *supreme power* of the community is vested." Mosheim, Ch. Hist. I. pp. 82, 143.

"Each communicant, as member of the Church, had the right of taking part in all the transactions of that body, especially in *the choice of the clergy*, and in the discipline of the Church." Augusti, in Coleman's Antiq. p. 60. See also chap. 5.

---

* View Soc. Worship, p. 210.

"In ancient times there was not any small Church which had not a suffrage in the choice of its pastor." Barrow on the Pope's Supremacy, Supp. 6, § 12.

"In the earliest government of the first Christian society, that of Jerusalem, not the elders only, but the whole Church, were associated with the Apostles." Waddington, Ch. Hist. p. 41.

"As it is plain, by the general epistles, that *all* Church power was in the *people*, so we find them, before these were written, exercising this power." Tindal, Rights of the Christian Church, chap. 4, § 46, quoted in Hanbury's Historical Memorials, I. p. 9. London, 1839.

"The discipline of Christian Churches was primitively popular." Harrington, Popular Government, B. 2, chap. 5.*

3. It is the right and duty of a Church to interpret for itself the laws of Christ, and to enforce obedience, on the part of its members, to the system of faith and practice which it derives from the word of God.

"The Socinians hold that, as the Scriptures are the rule of faith, the essential articles of faith are so few, so simple, and so easily gathered out of clear explicit passages, that it is impossible for any man

---

* So also Hüllman, Kirchenverfassung, S. 21, 196. Curtis, Bib. Episc. p. 129. Burton, Church Hist., ch. 12, p. 262. Punchard, Hist. of Congregat. ch 10.

who has the exercise of his reason to miss them; that all mistakes and differences of opinion amongst those who search the Scriptures, respect points which are not essential, and concerning which it is both vain and hurtful to try to establish an uniformity of opinion; that it is in all cases a sufficient declaration of Christian faith to say that we believe the Scriptures; that no harm can arise from allowing every man to interpret the Scriptures as he pleases; and that, as Scripture may be sufficiently understood for the purposes of salvation, without any foreign assistance, all creeds and confessions of faith, composed and prescribed by human authority, are an encroachment upon the prerogative of the Supreme Teacher, an invasion of the right of private judgment, and a pernicious attempt to substitute the commandments of men in place of the doctrine of God. According to this plan, there is left to the Church, and its ministers, in their teaching, merely the office of exhortation." \*

Such is the substance of the argument against human creeds, against the right of a Church to maintain its own views of divine truth, and require a concurrence in them on the part of all who are received to its fellowship. This position of the Socinians, the effect of a violent reaction against the extreme doctrine of the Papists, on the subject of

\* Hill's Divinity, p. 754.

tradition and church power, has never received the sanction of the great body of Protestants, who have insisted, both by precept and practice, upon the right and duty of a Church to set forth the main articles of its belief, in what is usually called a confession of faith. This has been the practice of the Baptists, both in their primary organizations, as churches, and in their general combinations for the spread of the Redeemer's kingdom. The Baptists in Great Britain, through the elders and brethren of upwards of a hundred churches, put forth, in the year 1689, a confession of faith, generally known as the Century Confession, together with a Catechism for the use of the young. These were adopted by the Philadelphia Association, in this country, in 1742, and subsequently by the Charleston, Savannah River, and other Associations. As Associations are composed of delegates from the Churches, their acts merely expressed the will of these bodies. The General (Arminian) Baptists of Great Britain published their confession of faith in 1663.\*

---

\* The Century Confession was republished, with other valuable matter, by Rev. D. Sheppard, Charleston, 1831. It coincides in doctrine with the Westminster Confession, from which, indeed, it was taken; and this latter was designed to be an exhibition of the faith of English Protestantism. Vid. Dr. Smyth's Hist. Westm. Assembly, Sec. 2. The copy of the Baptist Catechism in my possession, which is in fact the Shorter Catechism of the Assembly, adapted to our own views, in certain particulars, was published in

The Century Confession embraces the following doctrines: — The unity of God; the existence of three equal persons in the Godhead; the just condemnation and total depravity of all mankind by the fall of our first parents; eternal, personal, and unconditional election; the proper divinity of the Lord Jesus Christ; the necessity of his atonement, and its special relation to the sins of the elect only; justification by the imputed righteousness of Christ alone; effectual calling; perseverance of the saints; believers' baptism by immersion only; the Lord's Supper, a privilege peculiar to baptized believers, regularly admitted to Church fellowship; the resurrection of the body and general judgment; the final happiness of the saints, and misery of the wicked, alike interminable; the obligation of every intelligent creature to love God supremely, to believe what God says, and practise what God commands; and the divine inspiration of the Old and New Testaments, as the complete and infallible rule of faith and practice.*

Charleston, S. C., 1813. The Confession of the General Baptists, entitled, "A brief Confession or Declaration of Faith, set forth by an Assembly of Messengers, Elders, and Brethren of the Baptized Churches," may be seen in Grantham's Christianismus Primitivus. London, 1678.

\* The above brief compend of doctrine was drawn up by the Rev. Dr. Dagg. The following document presents another very excellent digest of the Century Confession:

The reasons which are now assigned for departing from this time-honored custom, are not sufficiently cogent to justify such a course, especially as our churches are as much as ever exposed to the irruption of a lax or false theology. It has been observ-

### ARTICLES OF FAITH
*Of the Mississippi River Baptist Association, adopted October 2d, 1846.*

1. We believe in one triune God, the Father, the Son, and the Holy Ghost; the same in essence, equal in power and glory.

2. We believe the Scriptures of the Old and New Testament were given by the inspiration of God, and are the only rule of faith and practice.

3. We believe in the fall of Adam from original rectitude; in the imputation of his sin to all his posterity; in the total depravity of human nature, and in man's inability to restore himself to the favor of God.

4. We believe that God has loved his people with an everlasting love; that he chose them in Christ before the foundation of the world; that he called them with a holy and effectual calling; and, being justified alone by the righteousness of Christ imputed to them, they are kept by the power of God, through faith unto salvation.

5. We believe there is one Mediator between God and man—the man Christ Jesus, who, by the satisfaction made to law and justice, in becoming an offering for sin, hath, by his most precious blood, redeemed the elect from under the curse of the law; that they might be holy and without blame before him in love.

6. We believe that good works are the fruits of faith, and follow after justification, and are evidences of a gracious state; and that all believers are bound to obey every command of God from a principle of love.

ed by a writer who argues against "the propriety of having any human selection or compilation, as a standard of faith and practice ": — " If it be said that the compilation thus prepared contains what is in the Bible, the question comes up, why then form

7. We believe in the resurrection of the dead, and a general judgment; that the happiness of the righteous and the punishment of the wicked will be everlasting.

## GOSPEL ORDER.

1. We believe that the visible Church of Jesus Christ is a congregation of faithful persons, who have given themselves to the Lord, and to one another, by the will of God and have covenanted to keep up a godly discipline, agreeably to the gospel.
2. We believe that Jesus Christ is the head of the Church, the only Lawgiver; that the government is with the Church.
3. That Baptism and the Lord's Supper are Gospel ordinances, appointed by Jesus Christ, and are to be continued in his Church until his second coming.
4. That the immersion of the body in water, in the name of the Father, and of the Son, and of the Holy Ghost, is the only Scriptural way of Baptism, as taught by Christ and his Apostles.
5. That none but regularly baptized Church members, who live a holy life, have a right to partake of the Lord's Supper.
6. That it is the privilege and duty of all believers to make a public profession of their faith, by submitting themselves as subjects for baptism, and as members of the visible Church.
7. That it is the duty of every regularly organized Church to expel from her communion all disorderly and immoral members, and who hold doctrines contrary to the Scriptures.

the compilation? Why not use the Bible as the standard. Can man present God's system in a selection and compilation of some of its parts, better than God himself has done it, as a whole, in His own book? Suppose the legislature should select portions of the constitution of the State, and compile them into a book, and set it forth as the standard by which its laws should be made. Would the people allow it?"*

This objection proceeds upon an erroneous conception of the nature and design of a creed. It is not a compilation of *some* of the parts of God's system, nor does it consist of *select portions* of the Scriptures. It is a digest of the whole, presenting in a small compass, and in the shape of distinct propositions, the great principles which constitute the system of revealed truth. In the Bible, these principles are not merely exhibited, they are expounded and defended at large. Moreover, a creed is not intended to supersede the word of God, as the standard of faith and practice; for it derives its validity and authority solely from its agreement with that word. It is a standard or rule of faith only in a secondary sense, and only to those who adopt it as the exponent of their views. It does not create, it simply expresses the truth; and is to be viewed, not in the light of an authority but a testimony. The

* Dr. Johnson, Gospel Developed, p 197.

adoption of a creed on the part of a church indicates not what is to be, but what is already believed. It is an expression of its cordial reception of the truth, and "sets forth in order a declaration of those things which are most surely believed among" its members.\*

The right of a Church to frame for itself a summary of Christian doctrine is evident from the nature of its organization. If "two cannot walk together except they be agreed," much less can professors of Christianity constitute a harmonious and efficient body, unless they concur in their views of what Christianity is. If it be proper for them to have correct views, it is proper to express them; and if it be proper to express them orally, it is equally so to express them in a written form. Again, each member of a church is bound to bear his testimony to the truth. But with what show of reason can it be affirmed that a duty, which is incumbent on members of a Church, in an individual, is not obligatory upon them in a collective capacity?

---

\* Luke 1 : 1. A creed is not *norma normans*, but *norma normata*. It contains the very kernel and essence of the Scriptures — ipsa medulla scripturæ. Of confessions of faith it has been well said — non imprimunt nobis credenda, sed exprimunt a nobis credita. Twesten, Vorlesungen. I. § 21, S. 296. Or, as Turretine has it, they are *normæ secundariæ*, non veritatis sed, *doctrinæ* in aliqua ecclesia receptæ, quoniam ex illis quid cum ecclesiæ doctrina conveniat, quidve ab ea discrepet, perspici potest et dijudicari. Theol. Elenc. Loc. XVIII. Quæst. 30, § 9.

It has been proved that a Church is charged with the discipline of its members, in reference both to faith and to practice. In a case of discipline, who is to pronounce judgment — the Church, or the party accused? To this question there can be but one reply. The Church, in the exercise of its legitimate prerogative, is to decide as to what is truth, and what constitutes a departure from the faith. But if a Church possesses this right, when an offender stands arraigned before it, it must have possessed the right previously, — the right to define its views of Scriptural truth, and require its members to conform to the same. "It has been asked," says Andrew Fuller, "by persons who disapprove of all church proceedings, on account of difference in religious principles, who is to judge what is heresy? We answer, those who are to judge what is immorality, in dealing with loose characters. To suppose it impossible to judge what heresy is, or to deny that the power of so deciding rests in a Christian Church, is to charge the apostolic precept with impertinence." * Again: "If a Christian society have no right to judge what is *truth*, and to render an agreement with them in certain points a term of communion, then neither have they a right to judge what is righteousness, nor to render an agreement

* Works, II. p. 466 Boston, 1833.

in matters of practical right and wrong a term of communion." *

Such being the unquestionable right of a Church, it simply remains to show that there is an obvious propriety and duty in having "human compilations," or summaries of doctrine. "Whether the united sentiments of a Christian society be expressed in writing or not, is immaterial, *provided*, they be mutually understood and avowed. Some societies have no written articles of faith or discipline; but with them, as with others that have, it is always understood that there are certain principles, a professed belief of which is deemed necessary to communion." † It will be perceived that the *writing* of Articles of Faith is accidental, not essential, and involves no principle which is not implied in holding them.

In the decision of this question, regard must be had to the dictates of reason and the lessons of experience. Had the author of revelation been pleased to give us truth, in naked propositions, arranged with scientific symmetry, in a regular system, the necessity of framing such a system for ourselves would never have existed. But he has not so chosen; and in this respect, there is a beautiful harmony between nature and revelation, indicating that

---

\* Works, II. p. 630.
† Fuller, Works, II. p. 630.

both proceed from the same divine author. As in nature (to select a single example), the various vegetable productions which beautify the surface of the earth, and adorn the caverns of the sea, are not found arranged with reference to their respective genera and species, according to the classification of the botanist, but are scattered promiscuously over the globe, soliciting the labor of science to classify them, and rewarding it by unfolding new and glorious views of the wisdom, power, and benevolence of the Deity, so the truths of revelation, the several parts of a beautiful and glorious system, lie scattered over the pages of the Bible, to be gathered by the hand of pious diligence, and reared into a temple to the divine glory. This method subserves the purposes of moral probation and discipline; for the character of the system which each inquirer derives from the Bible depends, in a great measure, upon the moral qualifications with which he consults its sacred pages.

Were the results of such inquiries always the same, did the various bodies which profess our common religion hold the same sentiments, specific Articles of Faith might be dispensed with; but when it is remembered that these bodies, although they take their position upon a common platform — the word of God — profess diverse and even opposite sentiments, the necessity of such articles is evinced by the most plain and cogent considerations. Our Lord warned his disciples against false prophets, who would come in sheep's clothing, while inwardly they were ravening wolves. The Apostles witnessed the fulfilment of his predictions; and their epistles abound with complaints of false teachers, who corrupted the word of God, brought in damnable heresies, subverted whole houses, and wrested the Scriptures to their own destruction.* Against these, Christians are exhorted to "contend earnestly for the faith once delivered to the saints," and to be on their guard against "the sleight of men and cunning craftiness, whereby they lie in wait to deceive." † These and similar directions "teach clearly that an acknowledgment of the truth of Scripture is not a sufficient security for soundness of faith, because they state a perversion of Scripture by those who have received it, as not only a possible case, but as a case which then actually existed; and consequently they imply that it is lawful for the ministers of religion (and the churches) to employ some additional guard to that 'form of sound words,' which they are required to hold fast and defend." ‡ These observations expose the futility of the demand

---

\* Matt. 6 : 5.   2 Cor. 2 : 17.   2 Tim. 2 : 18.   Titus 1 : 11.   2 Peter 3 : 3–16.   1 John 4 : 6.
† Eph. 4 : 13.   Heb. 13 : 7.   Tit. 1 : 9.
‡ Hill's Divinity, p. 756.

which is sometimes made, that Confessions of Faith should be expressed in the language of Scripture, or in general terms. "The very purpose for which they are composed being to guard against error, it is plain that they become nugatory if they deliver the truths of religion in those words of Scripture which had been perverted, or in terms so general as to include both the error and the truth."\*

The only plausible objection which is urged against the use of human creeds as the condition of Church fellowship, is that it restricts freedom of inquiry, and interferes with the rights of conscience. "If," says Andrew Fuller, "a subscription to Articles of Faith were required without examination, or enforced by civil penalties, it would be an unwarrantable imposititition on the rights of conscience. But if an explicit agreement in what may be deemed fundamental principles be judged essential to fellowship, this is only requiring that a man appear to be a Christian, before he can have a right to be treated as such. Suppose it were required of a Jew or an infidel, before he is admitted to the Lord's Supper (which either might be disposed to solicit for some worldly purpose), that he must previously

---

\* Hill, p. 760. It is well known from the history of heresy, that the use of Scripture language, in a sense opposed to orthodoxy, is one of the most common disguises of errorists; and as to the use of general terms, it has been the refuge of heresy in all ages.

become a believer. Should we thereby impose Christtianity upon him? He might claim the right of private judgment, and deem such a requisition incompatible with its admission; but it is evident that he could not be entitled to Christian regard, and that, while he exclaimed against the imposition of creeds and systems, he himself would be guilty of an imposition of the grossest kind, utterly inconsistent with the rights of voluntary and social compact, as well as of Christian liberty." *

The use of a confession of faith, so far from disparaging the authority of the Bible, as a standard, really exalts it. It insists upon a correct interpretation of the word of God, a cordial reception of its truths, and an entire submission to its directions. A Church, rearing this rampart around the sacred volume, guarding every entrance with jealous vigilance, and carefully questioning every comer who essays to gain ad-

---

* Works, II. p. 629 – 630. "The persons most ready to bring forward this objection are those whose system excludes some of the doctrines which the great body of Protestants agree in receiving. In their manner of stating the objection, they are careful to conceal their disbelief of particular doctrines, under a zeal for liberty of conscience, and the right of private judgment; and instead of affirming that a confession declares what is false, they choose rather to say, that by the particularity with which it states the received opinion, it abridges and invades that freedom in every thing that concerns religion, which Christians derive from the spirit of the gospel." Hill, Divinity, p. 760.

mission under false colors and with "feigned words," protects the divine repository of truth against the insidious artifices of those who would corrupt it or handle it deceitfully. If they choose to wrest the Scriptures to their own destruction, the responsibility rests with themselves. The Church will never fraternize with them in their unholy designs, nor suffer them to pollute her sacred enclosure. Thus she fulfils her high mission as the "pillar and ground of the truth." As pillars, in ancient time, bore the written edicts of the potentates of the earth, "seen and read of all men," so the Church stands forth, with the great principles of divine truth graven upon her front,—the living, faithful witness of her invisible king.

Such are some of the reasons which justify the Churches in the use of definite articles of faith. The custom is thought by some inquirers into the usages of antiquity, to have been apostolical, or, at least, sanctioned by apostolic precedent. It is supposed that the sermon on the mount, which presents a digested system of Christian ethics, the Lord's Prayer, the use of the baptismal formula, and the allusion to a "form of sound words,"—all point to such an observance. But however this may be, we possess incontestible evidence that, soon after the age of the apostles, when the rise of heresies began to threaten the peace and purity of the Churches, it was deemed necessary to embrace the leading facts and principles of the Gospel in a compendious system, and present them, for concurrence or subscription, to candidates for baptism and church fellowship;* and in all succeeding times, the supporters of truth against error have deemed it their sacred duty to bear their explicit and unequivocal testimony, in terms which neither friends nor enemies could misinterpret; some of them, in circumstances in which a mere general assent to the truth of the Scriptures, would have saved them from the appalling agonies of martyrdom.†

The propriety of the course which has been adopted by Christian Churches, with reference to a formal enunciation of their distinctive principles, is illustrated and confirmed by analagous procedures in

---

* Coleman's Christian Antiq. p. 253. "From the earliest organization of the Church, some confession and rule of faith must evidently have been necessary. This rule of faith must have been derived from the teaching, either oral or written, of the apostles; and may have been earlier than the writings of the New Testament in their present form. Luke 1: 1—4. Gal. 1: 11. As the preaching of the Apostles preceded their written instructions, so an oral confession may have preceded a written one, comprising an epitome of the gospel. From such a source may have sprung the great variety of forms which were known previous to the council of Nice."

† Mosheim, Ch. Hist. I. chap. 3. Giescler, I. § 49. Münscher (Ed. Von Cöln), I. § 12. Barrow's Works (Am. Ed.), II. p. 569.

other bodies. Thus the government of the United States is administered, according to the provisions of a written constitution. Under this constitution different parties have arisen, sustaining the same relation to it which the various denominations of Christians sustain to the Scriptures. It is not deemed sufficient by any one of these parties, to require, on the part of its adherents, a simple subscription to the constitution; for this is the common basis of them all. Each party sets forth its own construction of the constitution, and states distinctly the principles upon which it is based. If an individual were to suffer himself to be chosen as a representative of one of these parties, and were then to betray their confidence, by giving his support to the measures of another, in vain would he plead in justification of his treachery, that the constitution was his political confession of faith; all parties alike would denounce him as a deceiver.

# CHAPTER VIII.

### INDEPENDENCE OF THE CHURCHES.

It has already been proved, that, according to the Scriptures, each Church of Christ is charged with the reception and discipline of its members, the election of its officers, and the general management of its affairs. This being the case, the independence of the Churches follows as a necessary consequence. The simplicity of this system of organization may not comport with the suggestions of human expediency. A more close and extensive combination, which should consolidate the Churches, fuse them into a compact and homogeneous mass, and centralize power in the hands of a select body, or of an individual, as the representative of sovereignty, may be preferred as best suited to develope and combine the energies of its component parts. But if this be the system which Divine wisdom has chosen, it is doubtless the wisest and the best. Experience has proved it to be so. It agrees best with the free spirit of Christianity, and is best adapted to the development of Christian life in the individual. It combines greater advantages, and is embarrassed with fewer difficulties, than any system which human ingenuity, pride, or the lust of power has ever devised.

## CHURCH POLITY.

It has been supposed that the transaction recorded in Acts 15, furnishes a precedent for a higher tribunal than a single independent Church. Writers on ecclesiastical polity have detected in the meeting at Jerusalem, a court of review, a synod or a general council, according to the bias with which they have, respectively, contemplated it. There is no just foundation for any of these suppositions. The case was altogether an extraordinary one. It sprung out of an exigency which could only occur in the incipient state of Christianity; and cannot, therefore, be pleaded in justification of subsequent assemblies, which undertake to legislate for the Churches, review their acts, and reverse their decisions. "In the above case there was no council of Churches held by their delegates. One Church sends messengers to ask information on a given subject. The answer is satisfactorily returned, and the instructions of the Holy Ghost are added concerning points of duty, in which all the Churches were interested. What assemblage of men, uninspired of God, can now say, " The Holy Ghost puts his seal to the decree which we send you, and you must keep it?" The above case then furnishes neither example nor authority for authoritative councils of Churches by their delegates."*

---

* Dr. W. B. Johnson. A Church of Christ, a Sermon, p. 26. Ripley and Barnes in loc. Curtis, Bib. Episc. p 131.

The independence of the Churches is attested by the highest authorities in Church history, as well as by many other distinguished writers.

"All the Churches in those primitive times were *independent* bodies; or none of them subject to the jurisdiction of any other. For, though the Churches which were founded by the apostles themselves, frequently had the honor shown them, to be consulted in difficult and doubtful cases, yet they had no judicial authority, no control, no power of giving laws. On the contrary, it is as clear as the noon-day, that all Christian Churches had *equal rights*, and were in all respects on a footing of equality. Nor does there appear in this first century, any vestige of that consociation of the Churches of the same province, which gave rise to *ecclesiastical councils* and to *metropolitans*. Rather, as is manifest, it was not till the *second* century that the custom of holding ecclesiastical councils began, first in Greece, and thence extended into other provinces." Mosheim, I. pp. 86, 142. cf. Gieseler, I. p. 103. King, ch. 8.

"Every Church had its own spiritual head or bishop, and was independent of every other Church with respect to its own internal regulations." Burton, Hist. Ch. p. 262, New York, 1839.*

---

* Dr. Burton is an Episcopalian. How different the language of another writer of the same Church, who has

"Every society of Christians formed within itself a separate and independent republic." Gibbon, 1, p. 273.

"It is certain that during the first century from the death of Christ, the several Churches which had been instituted by the apostles, or their successors, were entirely independent of each other." Tytler, Universal History, 2, p. 4. Guizot, Hist. Civilization, p. 52.

Some objections have been urged against the independent polity, which demand at least a passing notice. These are: —

1. It destroys the visible unity of the Church.* It has been proved, in a former chapter of this work, that the visible Church Catholic is a figment of the imagination, destitute of Scriptural authority. If this be the case, the objection possesses no weight. The only kind of ecclesiastical unity contemplated in the Scriptures can be as well secured among independent Churches as any others. The principle of Christian union is the law of love. This divine element pervades the bosoms of all true followers of the Redeemer, and unites the

ventured to assert that "the system of Independency is totally without the remotest support from either Scripture or Antiquity." Townsend, N. T. Part 4, note 2.

* Dick, Theol. 2, p. 491. Hill, p. 695. Smyth, Catechism, p. 103, where, also, may be found the other objections which are here examined.

various societies, into which they are divided, in one affectionate sisterhood. No other decrees are necessary to perpetuate this union, except the solemn command of their divine Master; and all attempts to effect the result by authoritative decisions of councils or coercive measures will prove abortive, or at best secure only a constrained and deceptive uniformity, the uniformity, not of faith and love, but of hypocrisy or servitude. Ecclesiastical systems, the growth of worldly policy, and stamped with the wisdom of human expediency, may *dove-tail* the Churches together, so as to present a vast and imposing visible confederation: the power of divine love alone can *weld* them in spiritual unity, and make them one family of Christ.

2. Another objection urged against our Church polity, is that it places too much power in the hands of the people. It is alledged that many Christian Churches are incapable of self-government; and one writer particularly deprecates, with pious fervor, the idea of "referring every decision to numbers and suffrages, and placing all that is good, and venerable, and influential among the members themselves at the feet of a *democracy*."\* It is readily admitted that the Bible system of Church govern-

---

\* R. Watson, Institutes part 4, chap 1. Mr. Wesley said: "We are no republicans;" and his followers seem content to repeat the confession.

ments is suited only to a Bible constituency.\* If churches are composed only of such as give credible evidence of having been taught by the Spirit of God, they may safely be entrusted with the management of their own interests. But when the door of admission is thrown wide open, and merely nominal professors are introduced, it becomes necessary to coerce and restrain them by powers higher than themselves; to curb them by courts and councils, or awe them by a hierarchy. It will generally be found that in proportion to the facility of admission into any Church is the stringency of its government. The Baptists recognize only believers as the constituents of a gospel Church and commit its government to its members. The Presbyterians, who, although they consider infants as "in some sort" members of the Church, yet exclude all but believers from full membership, are essentially republican in their form of government. They elect their own rulers. The Methodists receive applicants to their communion without the requisition of personal piety; and then excluding them from all participation in the government of the Church, rule them by clerical conferences. The Roman Catholics would cheerfully admit to the Church, by baptism, the whole human family, and then proceed to erect over them

---

\* Curtis, Bib. Episc., Lec. 6.

a ghostly tyranny, reducing them to due subjection by the rack, the stake, purgatory, and hell.

3. It is further alledged against the system of Independency, that it unfits the Church to perform, in her distinctive character, and through her own organization, her appropriate duty of extending the kingdom of the Redeemer throughout the world. To this it is sufficient to reply by an appeal to facts. The Churches of the New Testament were, as has been proved, constituted on this principle, and yet within a century after the death of Christ, they had pushed the conquests of his cross to the remotest limits of the civilized world. It is an indubitable fact that, in modern times, Churches founded on the principles of Congregationalism, gave the first impulse to the missionary enterprise; and they are, at the present moment, acting a conspicuous part in all the great religious movements of the age. Their sovereignty, as independent bodies, presents no obstacle to their coöperation in measures of common utility, in education, Bible and Tract distribution, and in general movements for the spread of the Redeemer's kingdom.

## CHAPTER IX.

#### OFFICERS OF A CHURCH.

The permanent officers of a Church are of two kinds: elders (who are also called pastors, teachers, ministers, overseers or bishops) and deacons.

The Scriptures furnish us with an enumeration of all the gifts which were bestowed upon the apostolic churches. They mention apostles, prophets, evangelists, pastors, and teachers; deacons, miracles, gifts of healing, helps, governments, and diversities of tongues.\* It is evident that many of these must have been extraordinary, designed to meet the peculiar exigences of Christianity in its incipient efforts for diffusion. That miraculous and prophetic gifts have ceased is unquestionable. So have others. It was the design of Christ to provide for only two permanent officers in the Churches, bishops and deacons.

It has been strenuously contended that the apostolic office is permanent, and that it is continued in a succession of Bishops who profess a superiority in ministerial power and rights over the elders and the Churches. The weakness of this assumption

---

\* 1 Cor. 12: 28: Eph. 4: 11. Neander, Apos. Church, ch. 5.

can be easily exposed. The qualifications of an apostle were such as none of their pretended successors can be shown to have possessed.

1. The apostles were witnesses of Christ. To qualify them for this important office, our blessed Lord selected the twelve as his personal attendants, communicated to them his plans and purposes, and made them the witnesses of his crucifixion, resurrection and ascension. These are the great facts upon which the Christian religion is founded. It was indispensable, therefore, that they should be sustained by the most clear and unimpeachable testimony. To bear this testimony, and thus lay the foundation of the glorious edifice of the Christian faith, was the primary and peculiar design of the apostolic office. "He ordained twelve, that they should be with him, and that he might send them forth to preach, and to have power to heal sicknesses and to cast out devils:"—Mark 3: 14; Matt. 10: 5. The same view is presented by Christ, after his resurrection. In his last interview with his disciples, he thus addressed them: "Thus it is written, and thus it behoved Christ to suffer, and to rise from the dead the third day; and that repentance and remission of sins should be preached in his name among all nations, beginning at Jerusalem. And ye are *witnesses* of these things." Luke 24: 45—48. So the Saviour spoke, and so the apos-

tles understood him. This is manifest from the words of Peter, when an apostle was about to be selected to fill the vacancy occasioned by the defection of Judas. "Of these men which have companied with us *all the time that the Lord Jesus went in and out among us*, beginning from the baptism of John, unto that same day that he was taken up from us, must one be ordained to be a *witness with us*, of his resurrection." — Acts 1 : 21, 22. That this was the distinctive character of the office, is further evinced by the account which is given of the labors of the apostles. "This Jesus hath God raised up, whereof *we are witnesses*." Acts 2 : 32 ; 5 : 32 ; 10 : 39 — 41, etc.

The representation which has been given of the apostolic office derives strong confirmation from the case of the apostle Paul. He was called to the apostleship after the ascension of Christ. He had not had, therefore, that opportunity for personal observation which was necessary to qualify him to be a witness of Christ. How was this defect supplied? By supernatural revelation. Christ appeared to him on his way to Damascus, and transformed a bitter persecutor into a noble and unflinching apostle of his cause. We have three distinct accounts of his conversion and of his appointment to the apostolate. In each of these the design of the office is stated. "The God of our fathers hath chosen thee," said Ananias to the future apostle of the Gentiles, "that thou shouldst know his will, and *see that Just One, and shouldst hear the voice of his mouth;* for thou shalt be his *witness* unto all men of what thou hast seen and heard." — Acts 22 : 14, 15. "I have appeared unto thee *for this purpose*, to make thee a minister and a *witness*." — Acts 26 : 16. This latter was the language of Christ to Paul in the original commission. That it was understood by the apostle himself in the manner in which it has just been represented, is manifest from his own subsequent appeal in 1 Cor. 9 : 2. In reply to those who challenged his claims to this high office, he asks most triumphantly: "Have I not seen Jesus Christ our Lord?" Nothing can be more clear than that to have seen Jesus Christ was an indispensable qualification for the office of the apostleship, and that its main design was to bear witness to the cardinal facts of Christianity.\*

2. The apostles were distinguished by special prerogatives, which descended to none after them ; receiving their mission directly from Christ. The

---

\* Barnes, Episc. Exam. p. 25. Curtis, Bib. Episc. Lec. 2. Punchard, p. 71. Smyth, Pres. and Prel. chap. 4. Haldane, chap. 7. Bacon, Manual, p. 32. Campbell, Eccl. Hist. Lec. 5. Even Townsend, an Episcopalian, says, that to be made "a witness of the resurrection with us" is equivalent to "being raised to the apostolate." N. T. part 9, note 2.

power of conferring the extraordinary gifts of the Spirit, and the knowledge, by inspiration, of the whole doctrine of Christ.

3. They were universal bishops; the whole of Christendom was their charge, and the whole earth their diocese.

4. We have full proof that no idea of succession to the office was entertained in their own age, or in the times immediately succeeding; for no one, on the death of one apostle, was ever substituted in his place; and when the original college became extinct, the title also became extinct. The apostles were the ambassadors of Christ. Having delivered their message, and committed it to writing for the future use of the churches, their office became obsolete at their decease, and it was unnecessary that successors should be appointed.*

A fatal objection to the notion of apostolic succession, and the consequences derived from it, consists in the fact, that no such succession can be established by historical evidence. The links of the chain are broken, and lost beyond the possibility of recovery. The transmission of apostolic grace is no longer practicable; for the wires of the mystic telegraph are disconnected, tangled, and, along a portion of the pretended line, nowhere to be found. The vanity of the episcopal claim to an uninter-

*Eph. 2: 20. Rev. 21: 14.

rupted apostolical succession has been happily exposed by Archbishop Whately.

"There is not a minister in all Christendom, who is able to trace up, with any approach to certainty, his own spiritual pedigree. The sacramental virtue (for such it is that is implied, whether the term be used or not in the principle I have been speaking of) dependent on the imposition of hands, with a due observance of apostolical usages, by a bishop, himself duly consecrated, after having been in like manner baptized into the church, and ordained deacon and priest; this sacramental virtue, if a single link of the chain be faulty, must, on the above principles, be utterly nullified forever after, in respect of all the links that hang on that one. For if a bishop has not been duly consecrated, or had not been, previously, rightly ordained, his ordinations are null, and so are the ministrations of those ordained by him, and their ordination of others (supposing any of the persons ordained by him to attain to the episcopal office); and so on, without end. The poisonous taint of informality, if it once creep in undetected, will spread the infection of nullity to an indefinite and irremediable extent.

"And who can undertake to pronounce, that during that long period, usually designated as the Dark Ages, no such taint ever was introduced? Irregularities could not have been wholly excluded, without a perpetual miracle; and that no such miraculous interference existed, we have even historical proof. Amidst the numerous corruptions of doctrine and of practice, and gross superstitions that crept in during those ages, we find recorded descriptions, not only of the profound ignorance and profligacy of life of many of the clergy, but also of the grossest irregularity in respect of discipline and form. We read of bishops, consecrated when mere children; of men officiating who barely knew their letters; of prelates expelled, and others put in their places by violence; of illiterate and profligate laymen, and habitual drunkards, admitted to holy orders; and, in short, of the prevalence of every kind of disorder, and reckless disregard of the decency which the apostle enjoins. It is inconceivable, that any one, even moderately acquainted with history, can feel a certainty, or any approach to certainty, that, amidst all confusion and corruption, every requisite form was, in every instance, strictly adhered to by men, many of them openly profane and secular, unrestrained by public opinion, through the gross ignorance of the population among which they lived; and that no one, not duly consecrated or ordained, was admitted to sacred offices."*

The attempt to prove that an order existed in

* Kingdom of Christ, p. 128. The argument is stated with great force, by Chillingworth. Chap. II. Answer, §§ 64—68.

the ministry of the primitive churches as successors to the apostles, and therefore superior to elders, proves a failure. We may therefore consider it as comprising only elders and deacons. These are all that the Head of the Church has embraced in its ordinary and permanent organization. Even these are not indispensable. The Church at Jerusalem was in existence some time before it was found necessary to institute the order of deacons; and many other churches seem to have had no officers of either description. Paul and Barnabas, in their first missionary excursion from Antioch, passed through Pamphylia, Pisidia, and Lycaonia, and planted churches. After the lapse of about four years, they returned through those regions, " confirming the souls of the disciples," and " ordaining them elders in every Church." Up to this period, therefore, there had been no elders in the churches. The same is true of other churches. It would seem, therefore, that "the officers of a church are not essential to its being, though they are to its well being."\*

The apostolic churches seem, in general, to have had a plurality of elders as well as deacons. The apostle addressed his epistle to the Church at Philippi " with the *bishops* and deacons;" sent for

---

\* Bacon, Church Manual, p. 35  Discipline, Charleston Association, chap. 2.  Walker, Church Discipline, § 2.

"the *elders* of the Church at Ephesus;" and Paul and Barnabas as well as Titus "ordained elders" in the churches of Asia Minor and Crete. It seems, therefore, a fair inference that this was their usual practice. Of the reason of it we are not informed; but the existence of the practice seems unquestionable. Perhaps the explanation given by Elsley and others is the most satisfactory. "In that age," he remarks, "Christians had no public edifices, but held their meetings in private houses. When they were numerous, these meetings, and the inspectors or bishops who presided over them, were multiplied in proportion."\* The number of officers, whether elders or deacons, necessary to the completeness of a church, is not determined in Scripture. This must be decided by the circumstances of each case, of which the party interested is the most competent judge.

A distinction has sometimes been made between teaching and ruling elders. This was formerly the

\*Annotation on the Gospels and Acts, p. 562 In proof of a plurality of elders see Haldane, ch. 7, p. 210—224.—Smyth, Name, Nature, &c., of Ruling Elders, p. 38. Coleman Primitive Church, chap. 6. Bacon, Manual, p. 39.—Wood's Lectures on Church Government, p. 50. Gieseler, Church History, 1, 29. Neander, Apostolic Church, p. 35, 92. Milman History Christ, p 194—199. "The plurality of ministers over the same church continued, even to the fourth century, to be the order of the churches." Planck Gesell, Verfass, 1, 551.

custom of Congregational churches, and obtains, at the present time, in the Presbyterian Church. For the support of this distinction, the passages of Scripture principally relied on are 1 Tim. 5 : 17 ; 1 Cor. 12 : 28.* The latter passage is too indefinite in its phraseology to establish the distinction, and would probably never have been supposed to contain it, had not an erroneous interpretation of the former passage previously led to the belief that such a distinction really existed. The passage in the first epistle to Timothy reads as follows: "Let the elders that rule well be counted worthy of double honor, especially they who labor in the word and doctrine." The attempt to establish the distinction in question on the authority of this passage, is encumbered with many and weighty difficulties. (1.) The appellation *elder* is, every where else, used to designate ministers of the Gospel. It is interchanged with *bishop*, and must therefore refer to the same officer. The qualifications necessary for a teacher are the same as those of presbyters. It was, therefore, foreign to the design of the apostle to draw the line contended for between ruling and teaching elders, and confine the members of each division to a particular sphere of duty.† That the

---

\* Calvin, Com. in loc. Smyth, Ecclesiastical Catechism, chap. 3, § 6. Miller, Presbyterianism, p. 58.

† 1 Tim. 3 : 2 ; Titus 1 : 9.

term elder is used only with reference to teachers or ministers of the Gospel, is conceded by many advocates of the Presbyterian polity.* (2.) The Scriptures connect teaching and ruling together as the appropriate work of those to whom the care of the churches is committed. "We beseech you to know them which *labor among you* and *are over you* in the Lord, and *admonish* you." These separate divisions of duty must be the province of the same officer, unless we suppose that an order has been instituted for the purpose of *admonishing* the Churches, as well as for ruling and teaching them. Compare Heb. 13: 7, 17, 24. (3.) The total absence of any directions with respect to the qualification of ruling elders, proves that no such officer is contemplated in the New Testament. If these are necessary to the completeness of Church organization, it is unaccountable, that while the other officers of the Church are plainly specified, and their qualifications enumerated, no provision should be made for ruling elders. On these grounds, we contend that an order of men in the Church, whose sole business is to assist the pastor in its government, is not warranted by the precept or practice of the apostles.

What, then, it may be asked, is the distinction to

---

* Smyth, Office of Ruling Elder, p. 48. Pres. and Prel. B. I. chap. 6.

which the apostle refers? The reply is obvious. It has been shown that a plurality of elders was customary in the apostolic Churches. Many of these, after the example of Paul, labored with their own hands for support; and as they were stationary, might do so with little inconvenience. Others felt impelled by the Spirit, to make missionary excursions into the contiguous settlements, and devote themselves to the preaching of the Gospel. While the apostle urges upon the Churches the duty of supporting all their elders, he commends to their *special* regard those of them who had consecrated themselves to this laborious and self-denying work. The distinction is not one of officers, but of duties belonging to the same office.*

An elder who devoted himself exclusively to the preaching of the Gospel in destitute regions, was termed an evangelist, a title which occurs only thrice in the New Testament. Acts 21 : 8; Eph. 4 : 11; 2 Tim. : 4, 5. Although not located in any particular place, he belonged to the Presbytery (or Bishops) of some particular Church, by whom he was sent forth to evangelize the nations, found Churches, and extend the kingdom of the Redeemer. As the religion of Jesus Christ is essentially aggressive, this class of ministers will be

---

* Punchard, Congregat. p. 81. Upham, Ratio Discipl. § 38. Pictet, Theol. Christ. Lib. XII. c. 10

needed until the world is converted to the faith. Modern missionaries have succeeded to the duties of the primitive evangelists.

A careful examination of the Scriptures has thus led us to the conclusion, that Christ has provided for his Churches only two classes of officers; bishops, or elders, and deacons. These officers are chosen by the people, and derive all their authority, under the Great Head of the Church, from the consent of the governed. Their position involves the most solemn responsibilities. It is their duty to provide for the welfare of the particular flock which has been committed to their charge; watch over and feed it with the bread of life, and minister to its comfort and security while on its journey to the celestial fold. They are not to lord it over God's heritage. Any attempt on their part to restrict the privileges of believers, to invade their just rights, and deprive them of the liberty with which Christ has made them free, should be firmly and steadfastly resisted by all who are interested in preserving the institutions of the Gospel, as the only Lord and Master has delivered them. "The ecclesiastical office," says Gros, "is a service of the Church *(ministerium)*, not a lordship *(imperium)*, over its members." \*
A hierarchy claiming a divine right of jurisdiction over the servants of Christ, is as alien to the spirit

---

\* Lehrbuch des Naturrechts. § 281.

of the Gospel, as it is hostile to their moral and spiritual interests. The growth of ambition, avarice, and corruption, its embrace is pollution and death.

## CHAPTER X.

#### IDENTITY OF BISHOPS AND ELDERS.

In examining the arrangements which Christ has made for the external development of his kingdom, we have seen that he has instituted only two officers in a Christian Church. In opposition to this, it has been maintained that bishops and elders (presbyters or priests) are different officers, that deacons are preachers of the Gospel, and hence that the christian ministry is composed of three orders: bishops, priests and deacons. This is the episcopal scheme. The nature of the deacon's office is shown in its appropriate place. It is my object in this chapter to prove that the Scriptures make no official distinction between bishops and elders, that these are only different appellations for the same officers. The position is sustained,

1. By the import of the terms, and their interchange by the sacred writers.

The term elder is of Jewish origin, and imports the wisdom and dignity of age, while the other term bishop, which was borrowed from Grecian usage, designates the object for which the office was instituted. "This name," says Robinson, "was, originally, simply the Greek term equivalent to *elder*, which latter was derived from the Jewish polity." * That this statement is correct, is evident from the usage of the sacred writers.

One of the most unequivocal passages relating to this subject is found in Acts 20 : 17, compared with v. 28. The apostle Paul, in his interview with the *elders* of Ephesus, addresses them in the following words : — "Take heed to yourselves, and to all the flock over which the Holy Ghost hath made you *overseers*, (or bishops,) to feed the church of God which he hath purchased with his own blood." Here the appellations are used interchangeably, the term bishop indicating the nature of the office to which elders are called.

Another passage equally clear occurs in the first chapter of Paul's epistle to Titus. "For this cause I left thee in Crete, that thou shouldst set in order the things that are wanting, [to the complete organization of the churches] and ordain *elders* in every city as I had appointed thee." Then in enumerating the qualifications of elders, he continues, (as if to show that elders and bishops were the same officers,) "For a bishop must be blameless, as the steward of God." †

---

\* Lex. N. T. p. 315; Neander, Apost. Church, B. 3, chap. 5, p. 92.

† In the postscrips to the epistles to Titus and Timothy, these evangelists are called bishops. But these

This position is still further confirmed by 1 Pet. 5 : 1—4. "The *elders* which are among you, I exhort, who also am an elder . . . Feed the flock of God which is among you, taking the *oversight* thereof, i. e. acting the part of a bishop."

The scriptural use of these terms is so clear that it has been conceded even by Episcopalians. "The name bishop, which now designates the highest grade of the ministry, is not appropriated to that office in Scripture. That name is given to the middle order, or Presbyters." * Every elder is, therefore, a bishop; and "were it not," as Milton has said, "that the tyranny of prelates under the name of bishops had made our ears tender and startling, we might call every good minister a bishop, as every bishop, yea the apostles themselves, are called ministers, and the angels, ministering spirits, and the ministers again angels."†

2. No intermediate officer is mentioned between

postscripts are spurious, not having been annexed to the epistles until the fifth century. "Certain it is that in the first three centuries, neither Timothy nor Titus is styled bishop by any writer." Campbell, Ecclesiastical History, Lecture 5, p. 79, where the absurdity of magnifying Titus into a metropolitan bishop is fully exposed.

* Bishop Onderdonk, Episcopacy Tested by Scripture, p. 12. Waddington, History Church, chap. 2, § 2. Bloomfield, N. T. note on Acts 20: 17. Maurice, Kingdom of Christ, p 370.

† Reformation in England. Wks.. p. 19.

bishops and deacons. The apostle, in his instructions to Timothy, 1 Tim. 3 : 1—7, after specifying the qualifications of a bishop, proceeds, immediately, to those of deacons. That this omission was not accidental, is evident from the fact that he afterwards alludes to the *presbytery*, 4 : 14. If these had constituted a separate grade in the ministry, he would certainly have given directions with respect to their qualifications. His omission to do so proves that, in his view, they were identical with bishops.

3. The qualifications of bishops and elders are the same.

In proof of this, it is merely necessary to consult 1 Tim. 3 : 2—7 : Tit. 1 : 6—10. The matter was so understood as late as Jerome ; for in speaking of these epistles, he remarks — "In both epistles, whether bishops or presbyters are to be elected (for with the ancients, bishops and elders were the same, the one being descriptive of rank, the other of age) they are required each to be the husband of one wife."*

4. Their rights and duties are the same.

If the terms, bishop and elder, are applied indiscriminately to the same person, it follows, of course, that whatever is ascribed in the Scriptures to the

---

* Ep. 83, ad Ocean, Coleman Primitive Church, p. 132.— Gieseler, Church History 1, § 29, note 1. Coleman. Christ. Antiq. p. 98.

one, appertains also to the other. But there is here an independent source of proof. The sacred writers, in describing the rights and duties of bishops in some passages, and of elders in others, employ language which shows that these were not different officers, but one and the same. Heb. 13 : 7, 17 ; 1 Thess. 5 : 12 ; 1 Tim. 5 : 17 ; 1 Tim 4 : 14 ; 2 Tim. 1 : 6, etc.*

There is scarcely a subject on which the testimony of antiquity is more uniform and explicit than the original equality of bishops and elders. A well known passage from Jerome has already been cited ; and many others might be referred to. It will be sufficient, however, to quote a few of them :

" It were a grevious sin to reject those who have faithfully fulfilled the duties of their *episcopal office*. Blessed are those *presbyters* (or elders) who have finished their course, &c." Clem. Epist. ad Cor. § 44.

"*Elders* who, with the succession of the *episcopat*, received the gift of truth." Irenaeus contr. haeres. IV., 26, § 2.

" There is no difference between a bishop and an

---

\* Coleman, Primitive Church, pp. 133 — 145. Barnes, Episc. Exam. pp. 130 — 133. The subject of this chapter is discussed, at large, by Dr. Smyth, in his Presbytery and Prelacy, B. I. Turretine, Theol. Elenc. Loc. XVIII. Quæst. 21.

elder." Aetius. ap. Epiphan. haeres. LXXV., p. 906.

To the same effect might be cited the testimony of Justin Martyr, Chrysostom, and others, but the limits of this work forbid it. The reader will find the passages in the works to which reference has been made above.

The best ecclesiastical historians and critics concur in the view which has been taken of the equality of bishops and elders.

"I can discover no other difference between the *elders* and *bishops* in the apostolic age, than that the first signifies the rank, the second the duties of the office, whether the reference is to one or more." Neander, Apost. Church, B. III. ch. 5, p. 92. Comp. Gieseler, I. § 29.

"The official designations, bishop and elder, had, in primitive times, the same signification." Hullmann, Kirchenverfassung, S. 17.

"It is most manifest that both terms are promiscuously used in the N. T. of one and the same class of persons." Mosheim, Church History, 1, p. 82.

To this view the Reformers were led, with great unanimity, by the study of the Scriptures. Even in England, Wickliffe and a host of others contended for the original equality of bishops and elders.* Dr. John Reynolds, an Episcopal divine, who, according

* Punchard, History Congregat. chap. 10,

to Calamy, "was universally reckoned the wonder of his age," asserted, in the year 1588, "that they who, for these five hundred years, have been industrious in reforming the Church, have thought that all pastors, whether called bishops or presbyters, have, according to the word of God, like power and authority." \*

The perfect parity of all the ministers of the Gospel, derives strong confirmation from the spirit which our divine Master enjoined upon his disciples. On that memorable occasion, when the weakness of a mother's partiality menaced the fraternal union of the chosen band, by a request, which, springing from unhallowed ambition, sought to exalt the sons of Zebedee to a position above their brethren, he interposed his counsel and authority, and taught them that the path to real greatness and glory lay through humility and self-abasement. He refused to recognize any distinction among his followers, except that which arises from their personal devotion to him and his servants. "Ye know that the princes of the Gentiles exercise dominion over them, and they that are great exercise authority over them. But it shall not be so among you: but whosoever will be great among you, let him be your minister; and

---

\* Punchard, p. 197. The sentiments of the Reformers are exhibited by Burnet, History Reformation; and Neal Hist. Puritans.

whosoever will be chief among you, let him be your servant. Even as the son of man came, not to be ministered unto, but to minister, and to give his life a ransom for many." He thus rebuked all aspirations after rank and power among his followers, summoned them to laborious and self-denying service as the only criterion of greatness in his kingdom, and incited them to the pursuit of substantial honor and influence, by his own spotless example.

## CHAPTER XI.

#### RIGHTS AND DUTIES OF BISHOPS.

The episcopate is an office; and involves, therefore, the possession of certain rights, and an obligation to perform specific duties. If this were not the case, the office would be superfluous, and the officer himself a shadow. As these rights and duties necessarily involve each other, it will be unnecessary to treat of them separately. An enumeration of the various functions which have been appropriated to the office of a bishop by inspired authority, will sufficiently indicate both his rights and his duties.

1. It is appropriate to this officer of a Church, to administer the rite of baptism. This is evident from the commission of the Redeemer to the apostles, in which the same persons are empowered to preach and to baptize. Those who were "added to the Church" on the day of Pentecost, were first baptized by the apostles. Philip baptized the eunuch upon his own authority, as a Christian minister; and Paul refers to the ordinance, as administered by himself, in such a manner, as to show that he considered that he alone was charged with the responsibility of the act. Every minister of the Gospel is

authorized, by the divine commission, to baptize. Although, for the sake of convenience, the applicant for the rite is examined before the Church, that the members may, at the same time, judge of his qualifications for Church membership, the authority to administer it rests with those to whom the commission of the Saviour has been delivered.

It is, therefore, the special duty of the minister to examine the applicant, carefully, with reference to all the points which are implied in a credible profession of faith in the Son of God. As one who watches for souls, it is incumbent on him to deal faithfully with those who seek baptism at his hands, and receive none who do not afford satisfactory evidence that they have "passed from death unto life." The temptation to relax the terms of admission to this sacred rite; to be satisfied with slight or equivocal evidence of a change of heart; and receive promiscuously all who apply, in order to augment the number of apparent converts and acquire the reputation of a highly successful preacher of the Word, is one to which no conscientious minister will ever yield.

2. Another prerogative of the bishop is the right to rule.

This officer of the Church is denominated an overseer—a ruler—terms which imply the exercise of authority in its government. 1 Thess. 5 : 12, 13 ;

Heb. 13 : 7, 17, 24 ; Acts. 20 : 17, 18, 28 ; 1 Tim. 5 : 17 ; 1 Pet. 5 : 1—3. This authority involves no legislative power or right; it is ministerial and executive.* It is of much importance to understand the nature of the subjection which is enjoined by Christ to the pastor of a Church. From misapprehension on this point, many offences have arisen in churches. A pastor, on the one hand, is persuaded that he is to rule; on the other hand, the people know that he is not to exercise lordship; and mutual jealousies arise. He thinks he is only contending for the legitimate exercise of an authority committed to him for the good of the Church. They, on the contrary, conceive that in opposing him, they are only maintaining their just rights, and resisting clerical encroachments. He deprecates the confusion which may ensue from the want of pastoral authority; they fear the evils which priestcraft has so often inflicted upon the servants of Christ.

"But when we turn to the inspired constitution of the Church, and ascertain that a pastor is to execute only the laws of Christ; that his power is restricted within these wholesome and well-defined limits,—all just grounds of jealousy are removed; he and his people are equally under obligation to the Redeemer. It is his duty to see that they obey, faithfully, the laws of his kingdom. He is to warn

---

* Dr. Johnson, Gospel Developed, p. 78.

and rebuke the disobedient, and, if they prove obstinate and perverse, to bring their cases before the Church, for its solemn adjudication. Should it be objected that this leaves the Churches without a government sufficiently effective for the preservation of peace and good order, the only answer that can be made, is that no other government is warranted by Scripture."*

In virtue of his position, as ruler of the Church, the pastor possesses the right to preside at all its meetings.

3. The pastor, or bishop, is entitled to a competent temporal support.

It is one of the most obvious principles of reason and justice, that the laborer is worthy of his hire. This principle is universally recognized, in reference both to religious and secular concerns, and has obtained among all nations; for even idolaters and pagans support the ministers of their religion. It was enforced, by inspired authority, in the law of Moses. The tribe of Levi was set apart to the special service of the Most High, denied an inheritance in the land, and committed to their brethren for support.†

---

* Haldane Soc. Worship. pp. 242—248. See an excellent sermon by Andrew Fuller, in his Works. II. p, 226. Boston: 1833.

† Num. 18: 20. Deut. 10: 8. 14: 27. 18: 1.

As the reason of this law is permanent in its character and equally applicable to all ages, the principle has remained unchanged, under the gospel dispensation. So the apostle argued, when he said to the Corinthians, "Do ye not know that they which minister about holy things [under the law] live of the things of the temple? And they which wait at the altar are partakers with the altar? Even so hath the Lord ordained that they which preach the Gospel should live of the Gospel." *

The apostle here informs us that the right of the pastor to just compensation for his services, rests upon a divine statute. Of the enactment of it, we have an account in Matt. 10 : 5—16. "The workman is worthy of his meat." This statute, originally applicable to the apostles, was afterwards extended to the seventy disciples ; † and Paul affirms that its obligation is perpetual, having reference to all, in every age, who are called to preach the Gospel. This law, or ordinance of our Lord, is clearly recognized in the teaching and practice of the apostles. "Let him that is taught in the word, communicate to him that teacheth in all good things." ‡

---

\* 1 Cor. 9 : 13, 14.
† Luke 10 : 12.
‡ Gal. 6 : 6.  1 Cor. 9 : 7—11.  16 : 17.  Phil. 4 : 15—20. 2 Cor. 11 : 8, 9.  1 Tim. 5 : 17, 18, where the word *honor* means reward, stipend, or wages.

It is clear from these passages, that a minister of the Gospel has a divine warrant for claiming an adequate temporal support; and to deny it, is to contravene an express ordinance of Christ. It is equally clear that he is entitled to nothing more than a support. He is to live of the Gospel, not to accumulate property, and acquire an inheritance among his brethren. Having food and raiment, he ought therewith to be content, and not make his sacred calling subsidiary to his worldly interests. *

The possession of this right, on the part of the preacher of the Gospel, involves the corresponding duty to give himself wholly to the ministry. He must preach, teach, and exhort; visit the people of his charge, especially the sick; be ready, at all times, to aid them by his counsel and advice; detach himself, as far as practicable, from all temporal concerns, and devote his time and labor to the care of souls.

It has been remarked, in a previous chapter of this work, that a plurality of elders was customary in the apostolic Churches. This, if not universal, was, at least, quite common. Some of these elders seem to have combined a secular occupation with their calling as Christian ministers. Others devoted themselves entirely to the work of the ministry. It

---

* Howell, on the Deaconship, chap. V. Haldane, p. 226. Gospel Developed, p. 86.

is probable that, at that early period, each Church needed several elders; whilst the poverty of its members generally, and the contributions which they were called upon to make to the relief of their persecuted and suffering brethren, at home and abroad, rendered them unable to furnish an adequate support for these elders. Hence, some of them resorted to secular pursuits for maintenance; and in thus adapting themselves to the exigency of the case, they followed the example of the apostles. The same course is lawful at the present day. The pastor of a feeble Church may properly derive his support, in part, from some secular avocation; but he is, in no case, to resort to it for filthy lucre's sake. On the other hand, every Church, if able, is solemnly bound to sustain its pastor, so that he may give himself "continually to prayer and to the ministry of the word."

# CHAPTER XII.

### THE DEACONSHIP.

Our blessed Lord enumerated among the evidences of his divine mission, the interesting and instructive fact, that "the poor have the Gospel preached unto them." There is much in the promises which it discloses, and the hopes which it inspires, to claim the attention of those upon whom the blight of poverty has fallen. It is not surprising, therefore, that a large proportion of the early converts to the Christian faith, were drawn from the humbler walks of life. In consequence of such an accession to the community of the disciples, a new sphere of labor was demanded; since, in addition to the care of their souls, some consideration was due to their physical necessities. To have left them to endure the pressure of poverty, without any attempt, on the part of their brethren, to lessen its burden, would have been a reproach to the benevolent spirit of the new religion. Hence provision was made for their relief and support.

Whilst the number of the disciples in Jerusalem was small, the apostles could perform all the duties which the care of the Churches imposed on them.

But when, in consequence of the rapid progress of the Gospel, the Church was greatly enlarged, a division of labor became necessary; and they requested the brethren to select suitable persons to attend to the disbursement of their charities. The reason assigned by them for instituting this new office was, "It is not reason that we should leave the word of God [the preaching of the Gospel] and serve tables."* A separation was thus effected between the spiritual and the temporal affairs of the church; and the supervision of the latter was entrusted to a body of officers denominated deacons.

This term, which is now appropriated exclusively to a particular officer of the Church, means a minister or servant; and was, originally, applied to servants of all classes, whether their department were temporal or spiritual. But as each of the other classes of servants was distinguished by some more specific appellation, the term deacon was afterwards employed to designate a particular officer of the Church, to whom the charge of its temporalities was committed. Hence it is the appropriate business of the deacons, to serve tables. The distribution of the bread and and wine at the Lord's Supper, in which

* Acts 6: 2. The brokers, or money-changers, sat upon tables, in the market or other public places. Hence the import of the expression, *serve tables*, is to take care of money affairs, to have charge of temporalities, alms, &c. Robinson, Lex. N. T., p. 830. Bloomfield, in loc.

they are now employed, is a mere matter of custom or convenience, and forms no part of the original design of the office.

The nature of the deaconship is thus defined, by the history of the origin of the office. The official duties of the deacons, are the opposite of those which are assigned to ministers; and the very object contemplated in the institution of the order, was to relieve preachers of the Gospel from the management of secular interests, by placing them under the direction of others. If, therefore, the deacon is also a preacher, as some contend, the matter rests precisely where it did before his appointment; and those who give themselves "to prayer and to the ministry of the word," are employed in serving tables contrary to the "reason" and practice of the apostles. It is, indeed, objected that Philip, "one of the seven," did preach and baptize; but this does not affect the argumunt; for as a deacon, he had no right to do either. The only legitimate inference from the facts of the case is, that he preached as a minister of the word, after he had ceased to be a deacon, and had been ordained an evangelist.[*] The two offices are incompatible. He could not have filled both at the same time."[†]

As the deaconship was not designed to meet a temporary exigency, but is suited to a state of

---

[*] Acts 21: 8.
[†] Smyth. Presbytery and Prelacy. B. I. chap. XI.

affairs which must subsist as long as there is a Church upon the earth, it is a permanent institution. The *reason* of the office remaining unchanged, the office itself must be equally immutable. Every Church must have a place of worship, a pastor to be supported, and poor members who need assistance. It is the duty of every Church to contribute to the spread of the gospel, at home and abroad. For all these purposes, money is needed; and it is the duty of the deacons to collect and disburse it. In many churches, the deacons neglect altogether the appropriate duties of their station, and satisfy their consciences with the discharge of an extra-official matter with which they have no special concern; the distribution of the elements at the Lord's Supper — as if the solemn ordination of men of rare qualifications, by the imposition of hands, contemplated no higher object than the handing round of bread and wine; a service which any member of the Church is competent to perform. This lamentable defection from the order established by the apostles has rendered the office of deacon, in many of our Churches, a mere nullity, if not a grievous incumbrance.

In the primitive Churches, the peculiarities of Eastern manners and customs * rendered necessary

---

* So also among the Greeks, according to the testimony of Cornelius Nepos, in the Preface to his Lives.

the employment of females in services similar to those of the deacons. These were styled deaconesses. They were aged women, usually widows. To these females reference is made in 1 Tim. 5 : 9, 10. "Let not a widow be taken into the number (that is of deaconesses) under three score years old," &c. Their qualifications are specified by the apostle in connection with those of deacons. 1. Tim. 3 : 11, "Even so must their wives be grave," &c. The Greek term which our translators have rendered "*wives*," is supposed by the best interpreters to refer to deaconesses, and should have been rendered "the females." \* The expression cannot refer to the wives of deacons or of ministers, because they do not stand in any official relation to the Church.†

In occidental countries where no such restriction is imposed upon the intercourse of the sexes, this class of servants is unnecessary. Hence it has fallen into desuetude. "Morinus offers several reasons for the abrogating of this office in Syria, which were briefly, that the services of the women became less important after the cessation of the *agapae* of the primitive Church, — that the care of the sick and the poor, which had devolved upon the Church

---

\* Macknight and Bloomfield in loc.

† The existence of such a class is illustrated by Pliny, in his letter to Trajan, who calls them ministrae  Ep. Lib. X. p. 96. Comp. Romans 16 : 1 ; Timothy 5 : 3 ; Titus 2 : 2 ; Phil. 4 : 3.

was in the time of Constantine assumed by the State, — that after the introduction of infant baptism, their attendance at this ordinance became of less importance—and finally, that they, in their turn, became troublesome aspirants after the prerogatives of office; in a word, the order was abolished because it was no longer neccessary."* These helps were needed only for a time. The circumstances which required them have passed away; and as they sustained no official relation to the Church and were not embraced in its regular and permanent organization, no such class exists at the present day.†

* Coleman Christ. Antiq. p. 118. Punchard p. 85. Neander Ch. Hist. p. 108. Apos. Ch. B. 3, chap. 5, p. 97. Haldane, p. 227 — 235.

† On the subject of this chapter see King, Prim. Church, chap. 5, § 1. Hülmann, Kirchenverfassung, S. 15. Bacon Manual, p. 40. Punchard, pp. 92, 10. And for a thorough discussion of the whole subject, Howell, On the Deaconship. Phila, A. B. P. S. 1848.

## CHAPTER XIII.

ORDINATION.

It is the practice of all societies, ecclesiastical as well as civil, to induct persons into office by a solemn and formal inauguration. In reference to the officers of a Church, this ceremony is called ordination; although the word properly implies the whole of the transaction by which an individual is authorized to discharge official duties. To render it complete, two things are necessary, the choice of the Church, and the imposition of the hands of the Presbytery, with prayer and fasting. It has already been proved that a Church possesses the right to elect its own officers; and from this principle it has been inferred by some, that election is equivalent to ordination, and comprehends all that is included in that ceremony. The act of the Presbytery is therefore superfluous. If this were the case, and ordination were complete without the intervention of the Presbytery, there would have been no propriety in affirming, as the Scriptures do, that Paul and Barnabus "ordained elders in every church," &c.* In the efforts which have been made to sustain this position, great

---

* Acts 14 : 23 ; cf Tit. 1 : 5.

stress has been laid upon the term ordain, which signifies simply to appoint ;* but from the mere use of the term, nothing definite can be inferred, since it may relate to one kind of appointment as well as another. What we are inquiring after is the thing —the entire transaction which is included in the ceremony to which the term ordination is applied. This embraces the act of the Presbytery, as well as the act of the Church. Upon no other supposition can the different accounts which are given of the ceremony in the New Testament, be harmonized. In some cases the Church is said to ordain, or appoint, its officers ; in others, the Apostles are represented as doing the same thing. All this is in accordance with an obvious figure of speech, by which a part is put for the whole ; the initiatory or the consummating act, in this case, being employed to designate the entire transaction. The same rhetorical figure is used by the sacred writers on other subjects. Thus, the Lord's Supper is called breaking of bread ;† we are said to be justified by the blood of Christ, by his righteousness, by faith, by grace. The use of one of these terms does not exclude the others ; in each case a part is put for the whole. On a subject of such importance as this, I am happy to avail myself of the concurrence of Dr.

* Gospel Developed, ch. xii—xv.
† Acts 2 : 42 ; 20 : 7.

Howell, in the following observations, which are equally philosophical and scriptural. "In the government of states, whatever its form, checks and balances between the several departments are, by experience, found to be necessary to secure the interests of the parties concerned. They have, accordingly, been adopted by all civilized nations. In the Church of Christ they are instituted by divine authority. We have now before us a striking example. The ministry have no right to ordain any man to the Deaconship, not previously elected by the Church to that office. The consent of the Church is positively necessary, otherwise he would be a deacon "at large," having no place in which to exercise his functions. On the other hand, though brethren may be elected by the Church, they are still, unless ordained by the ministry, not deacons. There must be a concurrence between the Church and the ministry to create the officer. True, they do commonly concur, but not always, nor is it by any means a matter of course. Similar checks and balances exist with regard to the ordination of pastors and evangelists, and the baptism of candidates for membership in the Church. [That is, the minister may baptize, but the Church is not on that account bound to receive the candidate to membership.] Thus a double guard is thrown around all the most important interests of the kingdom of the Messiah."\*

The imposition of hands is a very ancient custom, and was practised for various purposes. It was symbolical of benediction, consecration, healing, and the gift of the Holy Spirit. Its import, when employed in ordination, may best be learned from the case of the Levites, noticed in Num. 8 : 10. It is well known that the tribe of Levi was consecrated to "the service of the Lord," in the place of the first born of all the children of Israel. To indicate this consecration, the following ceremony was commanded, "Thou shalt bring the Levites before the Lord, and the children of Israel shall put their hands upon the Levites. And Aaron shall offer the Levites before the Lord for an offering of the children of Israel, that they may execute the service of the Lord." A similar practice was observed when any thing was dedicated or consecrated to the Lord. There is nothing mysterious or magical in this ceremony. The children of Israel put their hands upon the Levites, to indicate by this symbolical act, that they gave them to the Lord. Such is its import in ordination. The laying on of the hands of the Presbytery, in the case of a person who has been chosen to office by the suffrages of the Church,

---

\* The Deaconship, p. 65 ; King. Prim. ch . p. 1, ch. 3–4 ; Crowell, Church Member's Manual, p. 106. Boston, 1847.

means nothing more than that his brethren have set him apart to a specific service. It is a public and authentic declaration of the fact. As such, it was observed by the primitive Churches. When the deacons were appointed, the Apostles prayed and laid hands on them, thus ordaining or appointing them to the office.* If employed in the ordination of deacons, it certainly must have been in that of elders; and the Scriptures furnish sufficiently clear indications that this was the case. 1 Tim. 4 : 14 ; 5 : 22. As the Apostle in the latter passage is speaking of elders, it is plain that he alludes to their appointment.

"It is evident," says Haldane, "that laying on of hands was used in separating men to the ministry in the primitive Apostolic Churches. It was not confined to occasions on which the Holy Ghost was conferred. It was used in ordaining elders and deacons who required only the ordinary gifts. There is nothing in the word of God setting aside this usage. It ought, therefore, to be observed where this can be done, according to the example given us in Scripture."†

The abettors of prelacy, dividing the ministry into three grades, restrict the power of ordination to the highest—the episcopal. But the Scriptures, as

\* Acts 6 : 6.
† Social Worship, ch. viii. p. 254; Smith, Presbytery and Prelacy, B. 1, ch. vii. § 2 ; Coleman, Prim. ch. p. 140.

I have before proved, furnish no authority for such grades. With them, bishop and elder, or presbyter, are only different designations of the same officer; and therefore no provision is made for the possession of this power by one class of ministers, to the exclusion of the rest. As to the notion that some mysterious virtue—some magic fluid—is transmitted in ordination, that the Holy Ghost is conferred upon the subject of it, to be conveyed by him to his fellow-men by means of the sacraments, it is utterly unscriptural and absurd; and can subserve no other purpose except the exaltation of the priesthood, and the tyranny of ecclesiastical domination.*

* Smyth, Presb. and Prel. B. I. ch. vii.-x.; Apostol. Succession, Lec. xx. note A; Coleman, Prim. ch. pp. 176–198; Dr. Woods, Objections to Episcopacy, Lec. IV.; King, Prim. Ch. P. I, chap. 3; Fuller's Works, II. p. 660.

## CHAPTER XIV.

### BAPTISM.

CHRISTIANITY is preëminently a spiritual religion. Its germination and growth in the heart are dependent upon the influence of the Holy Ghost. The external means of grace possess no intrinsic efficacy, but derive their tendency to confirm and strengthen the saints solely from the appointment of God. None of them are invested with the agency of an *opus operatum*, a power to convey grace by their inherent efficiency. This is particularly true of the Christian ordinances. They sustain no direct relation to the salvation of the soul; since the great transformation of character which is necessary to qualify for the bliss of heaven, must have been experienced before an individual is prepared to receive them. They are not saving ordinances; they can be approached by those only who are among the number of "such as shall be saved."

The New Testament contains traces of only two Christian ordinances. These are Baptism and the Lord's Supper. Of the two, the latter alone is strictly a Church ordinance. A Church is composed of baptized believers. Baptism is indispensable to their admission into it, but it does not make them Church members. The ordinance itself will now claim our attention.

In the prosecution of this inquiry, it will be necessary to determine what is baptism, and who are the subjects of the ordinance.

I. To a devout mind, it cannot be a matter of trivial interest, that the ordinances of the gospel not only derive their validity from the appointment of the great Head of the Church, but are hallowed and commended to our imitation by his own example. It would seem, therefore, that the sole object of a conscientious inquirer, would be to ascertain what was the form of the ordinance which was sanctioned by Christ himself. This having been determined, no other inquiries need supervene. The path of duty is plain. Having clearly discerned the footprints of his divine Exemplar, the Christian should wait for no additional incentives to "follow his steps." That Christ was baptized only in one way, is an obvious inference from the fact that he was baptized only once. This way it is important to ascertain. A serious and careful examination of the subject is demanded by the highest considerations; and the temper of indifference which passes it over, as a matter of little moment, can claim no fellowship with the spirit of Him who has taught us by his own example, to "fulfil all righteousness."

There is another aspect of this subject which claims our most profound consideration. Baptism is a positive institution. "Moral precepts," says Bishop Butler,\* "are precepts, the reason of which we see; positive precepts, are precepts, the reason of which we do not see. Moral duties arise out of the nature of the case itself, prior to external command; positive duties do not arise out of the nature of the case, but from external command; nor would they be duties at all, were it not for such command, received from Him whose creatures and subjects we are." The obligation to obedience, in either case, is the same; but the grounds upon which it rests are different. It is, moreover, the peculiarity of a moral precept, that it may be obeyed, when only the spirit of it is complied with. But in reference to a positive precept, no such distinction exits. Positive institutions derive their validity solely from the authority of the law-giver. They are obligatory, because he has made them so; and they are valid only in the form in which he has thought fit to appoint them. To mutilate or abridge them, is not simply to modify, but to subvert them.

If, therefore, the ordinance of baptism is a positive institution, resting upon the supreme will of the Head of the Church, and that will is expressed in positive commands, the obligation to a strict compli-

\* Analogy, P. II. Chap. 1.

ance with them cannot be denied. To alter the ordinance, or substitute any thing else in its place, is not to obey the command of Christ; and such a procedure involves either a reflection upon his wisdom, or a contempt of his authority. It is universally conceded, that the use of water is essential to Christian baptism. Immersion in any other liquid, although impregnated with the costliest perfumes, and rolling, like the fabled Pactolus, over a bed of gold, would not be Christian baptism. But in a positive ordinance, such as this, we have as little right to change one part as another, to determine the quantity as the quality of the liquid to be employed in its administration. It is manifest, therefore, that there cannot be several modes of baptism. Baptism is itself a mode; the word defines the ordinance; and in making a profession of religion, the use of water in any other mode than immersion, is a counterfeit of man's devising, and not a Christian institution.*

That immersion alone is baptism, is proved,

1. By the primary and ordinary meaning of the term. The founder of a system of religion, in communicating it to mankind, would doubtless select a medium of communication sufficiently clear and explicit to convey his meaning to those for whom that

---

* Westlake, Gen. View of Bap. chap. 1. Booth, Pedobap. Exam. P. 1, chap. 1. Carson on Bap. Preface.

system was designed; and as the Greek language is the chosen medium for the commuication of the Christian revelation, it is proper to inquire whether, upon the supposition that immersion is baptism, this language contains a word that conveys distinctly and clearly that meaning. The copiousness of the Greek tongue, and its wonderful adaptation to the expression of the minutest shades of thought, have often excited the admiration of the scholar. It would, therefore, be exceedingly strange if it lacked a term for the expression of so simple an idea as immersion. This, however, is not the fact.

There is a Greek verb, the primary and usual import of which, is to dip or immerse; and the corresponding noun signifies immersion. Of this fact we have evidence the most abundant and conclusive. I proceed to adduce some portion of it, confining myself to those who are not baptists in practice.

Robinson Lex. N. T. *Baptizo*, to immerse, to sink.

Donnegan Greek Lex. *Baptizo*, to immerse, submerge.

To the same effect is the testimony of Leigh, Schoettgen, Parkhurst, Stephanus, Pasor, Scapula, Hedericus, Wall, Bretschneider, and other Greek lexicographers.

Booth and other writers have collected together a cloud of witnesses on this point. I shall cite only a few of them, adding some others which I have met with in my own reading.

Witsius. It cannot be denied that the native signification of the word *baptizo*, is to plunge or dip Œcon. Fœd. IV. : 16, 13.

Salmasius. Baptism is immersion, and was administered, in ancient times, according to the force and meaning of the word. Now it is only *rhantism*, or sprinkling; not immersion, or dipping.

Prof. Stuart. *Bapto* and *baptizo*, mean to dip, plunge, or immerge, into any thing liquid. All lexicographers and critics of any note agree in this. Bibl. Repos. 3; p. 298.

Gomar. *Baptismos* and *baptisma*, signify the act of baptizing; that is, either plunging alone, or immersion and the consequent washing.

Buddeus. The words *baptizo* and *baptismos*, are not to be interpreted of aspersion, but always of immersion.

Vitringa. The act of baptising, is the immersion of believers in water. This expresses the force of the word,

Hospinian. Christ commanded us to be baptized; by which word it is certain immersion is signified.

Casaubon. This was the rite of baptizing, that persons were plunged into the water, which the very word *baptize* signifies.

Bossuet. To baptize, signifies to plunge, as is granted by all the world.

Turrettine. *Baptizo*, to baptize; to dip into, to immerse.\*

Bland. The metaphor of baptism, or immersion in water, or being put under floods, is familiar in Scripture, to signify a person overwhelmed with calamities. Annot. on Matt. I.; p. 43. Cambridge. 1828.

Elsley. Immersion in waters, or under floods; called here (Matt. 20: 22) baptism. Annot. p. 193. Oxford. 1844.

It is thus apparent, that the primary and ordinary meaning of *baptizo*, is to immerse. This being the case, the burden of proof is shifted upon those who affirm that it means something else; since it is an acknowledged principle of interpretation, as laid down by Ernesti, that "the literal meaning is not to be deserted without reason or necessity." This necessity must be plain and imperative; and even if cases could be cited in which the word, in its secondary meaning, is susceptible of a different interpretation, this fact would not invalidate the evidence which sustains its primary and usual import. This remark is peculiarly applicable to those cases in which the word is employed in a figurative sense.

\* Booth Pedobap. Exam. P. I., chap. 2. Hinton Hist. Bap. page 55.

The figure is to be explained by the meaning of the word, and not the meaning of the word by the figure.\*

But the advocates of immersion take a higher position than is implied in the suppositions which have just been made. Dr. Carson has proved by an array of facts and a conclusiveness of argument, not to be resisted, that "*baptizo* not only signifies to dip or immerse, but that it never has any other meaning." † In this position he is sustained by Prof. Stuart.‡

2. Circumstances attending Baptism.

A consideration of the circumstances attending the administration of this ordinance, confirms the opinion which has been expressed with respect to the import of *baptizo*. They are such as comport most naturally and fully with the idea of immersion. No necessity exists for departing from the original and proper meaning of the word. Let us consider some of them.

Matt. 3 : 16. Jesus, when he was baptized, went up straightway out of the water. The most obvious import of the phrase here employed is, that Jesus came up out of the water into which he had descended for the purpose of being baptized.

\* This common sense principle of interpretation, is recognized by Daehne Paulin. Lehrbegr. S. 93.

† On Baptism; pp. 13, 79. N. Y. 1832.

‡ Bibl. Repos. 3; pp. 292, 293.

John 3 : 23. John was baptizing in Enon, near to Salim, because there was much water there : and they came and were baptized.

That the phrase "much water," is equivalent to an abundance, or large body of water, and not to many rivulets, is evident from the usage of John, in other portions of his writings. Examine Rev. 1 : 15; 14 : 2; 19 : 6. It is obvious, that in these passages the sacred writer had reference to an abundant mass of water. Compare Rev. 17 : 1, 15. On this point, a learned Episcopalian remarks, "That the baptism of John was by plunging the body, seems to appear from what is related of him; namely, that he baptized in Jordan : that he baptized in Enon, because there was much water there; and that Christ being baptized came up out of the water; to which that seems to be parallel. Acts 8 : 38. Philip and the eunuch went down, &c."*

The case of the Ethiopian eunuch is equally decisive, in reference to the external act of baptism. Acts 8 : 36—39. "They went down both into the water, both Philip and the eunuch." For what purpose Philip went down into the water, unless to immerse the eunuch, it does not appear. The obvious and natural interpretation of the entire transaction coincides with the idea of immersion.

I might proceed to the examination of all the

* Bland, Annot. on Matt. I. p. 74.

cases in the New Testament, in which the circumstances attending the rite are detailed. But it is not necessary. If *baptizo* means to immerse, and is never used in any other sense, an actual immersion must have taken place in all the cases in reference to which it is used. I have cited the instances above, merely to show that the circumstances connected with the rite, harmonize most naturally and clearly with the meaning which is invariably ascribed to the word by the highest authorities in Greek philology and criticism. For a more extensive discussion of the subject, the reader is referred to the works mentioned in the margin.*

3. By the meaning of the ordinance.

Baptism is symbolical. It is expressive of certain great facts or truths which are essential to the Christian system; and so beautifully and appropriately does it represent the sublime central fact of our religion, the resurrection of the Redeemer, and its cardinal doctrine, the spiritual renovation of man, that even in the absence of any inspired teaching on the subject, the mind would naturally associate it with these fundamental truths. But the Scriptures have not left us to conjecture on this point. They furnish plain and explicit intimations that such is the design of this significant hieroglyphic of the

* Ripley, Exam. of Stuart, pp. 62—15. Carson, Jewett. Hinton, and Hague.

Christian economy. They teach us that baptism is an emblem of the resurrection of Christ, involving, of course, its immediate antecedents, his death and burial; and of that moral death and resurrection, which defines the character of his true followers. This is clearly the import of Rom. 6 : 4 ; Col. 2 : 12 ; 1 Pet. 3 : 21.

A few modern interpreters, among whom are Hodge and Stuart, deny that there is any allusion to the external act of baptism in Rom. 6 : 4 ; but in this they are at variance with the great body of commentators, as well as with the manifest import of the passage itself.

Macknight. He [Christ] submitted to be baptized, that is, to be buried under the water by John, and to be raised out of it again, as an emblem of his future death and resurrrection. In like manner, the baptism of believers is emblematical of their death, burial, and resurrection.

Bloomfield. There is a plain allusion to the ancient custom of baptism by immersion.

Leighton. Where the dipping into the water is referred to, as representing our dying with Christ ; and the return thence, as expressive of our rising with him. Comm. on 1 Pet. 3 : 21.

Hammond. It is a thing that every Christian knows, that the immersion in baptism refers to the death of Christ. The putting of the person into the water, denotes and proclaims the death and burial of Christ.

Hoadley. If baptism had been then performed as it is now amongst us, [the Church of England] we should never have so much as heard of this form of expression, of dying and rising again in this rite.*

The practice of immersion is commended to the disciples of Christ, by the symbolical exhibition which it makes of his own sublime and consummating act of grace. With inarticulate, yet expressive and touching power, it speaks of Him "who was delivered for our offences, and was raised again for our justification." It is sad to reflect that Christian hands have mutilated and disfigured this beautiful ordinance, and deprived it of its emblematic import; so that in our efforts to reinstate it in its original honor, and restore it to its primitive form, we have to contend, not with the enemies, but the friends of our common Lord. I would ask every pious, unimmersed reader who may peruse these pages, to pause, and ask himself, whether he is not lending his influence to overthrow one of the most significant monuments of the Saviour's resurrection. If immersion be emblematic of a truth so dear to the believer; if it so truthfully represents his own "washing of regeneration and renewing of the Holy Ghost," shed

* Works III. 890. Hague, Bap. Ques. 107. Crowell, Church Member's Manual, 152.

on him " abundantly by Jesus Christ, our Saviour; " and if, moreover, as Dr. Wall concedes, " it was, in all probability, the way by which our blessed Saviour, and for certain was the most usual and ordinary way by which the ancient Christians did receive their baptism," what should prevent all the friends of Christ from uniting their suffrages in its behalf, and combining to uphold and perpetuate this noble institution of our common Christianity? It affords matter of devout gratitude to God, that recent events present cheering indications of a return to scriptural baptism. The affusion of adults has become an exceedingly rare occurrence; they almost invariably demand immersion; and if infant baptism —which, by forestalling inquiry, perpetuates error— were abolished, this emblematic rite of the New Testament would stand forth in its primitive symmetry and beauty.*

4. Practice of the Primitive Churches.

The earliest uninspired records of ecclesiastical history, labor under the disadvantage of being justly suspected to be, to some extent, spurious, corrupt, and interpolated. Their evidence, therefore, is to be received with caution. It is clear to all who have examined the writings of the apostolic fathers, in connection with the productions of the evangelists and apostles,

* Booth, Ped. Exam. Part I. ch. 3, ch. 6. Westlake, ch. 3, 4.

that their views of Christian truth are entitled to very little consideration. But the allusions which their writings contain to the ordinance of baptism, where the genuineness of the passages themselves is admitted, may be safely credited; for as baptism is an external act, appealing to the senses, the testimony of an honest and unsuspected spectator of the ordinance, is all that we require or have a right to demand. It is on this principle, that we unhesitatingly reject the notions of the fathers, with reference to the efficacy of baptism; while we yield our unsuspecting assent to their testimony, with respect to the external act. The following passages disclose to us the practice of the early Churches:

Barnabas. Ep. ch. 11. We descend into the water, and come out of it.

Hermas. Pastor, 3. Men descend into the water, but ascend out of it.* Vid. also, Herm. Simil. IX. 16. Iren. III. 17, 2.

The testimony of later writers is equally explicit, and is moreover free from all suspicion.

Justin Martyr, (†164) towards the conclusion of his, so-called, Second Apology, thus alludes to the administration of the ordinance: "Those who believe and are persuaded that the things we teach and inculcate are true, and who profess ability thus to live, are directed to pray, with fasting, and to ask of

* Augusti Denker, VII. 77, remarks: "This passage contains distinct evidence of the custom of immersion."

God the forgiveness of their former sins, we also fasting and praying with them. Then we conduct to a place where there is water; and they are regenerated [baptized] in the manner in which we have been regenerated [baptized;] for they receive a washing with water, in the name of the Father." &c.*

Tertullian (†220.) We are immersed in water. Adv. Prax. 26. De cor. mil. 3.

Conc. Tolet. V., (A.D. 633.) The immersion in water is, as it were, the descent to Hades, and the emersion from the water, the resurrection.

It is thus clear that the practice of immersion continued in the Churches, from the age of Justin Martyr down to that of the Council of Toledo. It would be easy to cite other intervening witnesses, such as Clement of Alexandria, Cyril of Jerusalem, Basil, Gregory Nyssen, Chrysostom, Theodoret, Theophylact, Ambrose, &c.; but the above are sufficient to establish the general custom. During this period, immersion was the universal practice, except in cases of dangerous sickness. In such circumstances, pouring or sprinkling was tolerated by some of the

---

* I have given the translation of Dr. Murdock, in his edition of Mosheim, I. 167. Prof Emerson, of Andover, more correctly renders the last clause " for they then perform the ablution in the water." Christian Rev. VI. 305. The original may be seen in Münscher, Dogmengesch. (Von Cöln) I. § 99.

Churches; but neither of these was ever supported on the ground of tradition or apostolic practice. Cyprian, the great advocate and apologist of affusion, as the substitute of baptism, never pretended to place it upon the only ground upon which it could securely rest — primitive practice — but attempted to justify it by the " pressing necessity " of the case. In his judgment, baptism was necessary to salvation, and hence, he concluded that " God's indulgence " would permit an abridgment of the ordinance, in the cases of those whom sickness prevented from submitting to it in the usual form.\*

This position is maintained by the most learned and impartial historians. Eusebius informs us that when Novatian received baptism, by pouring, he was " attacked by an obstinate disease, and supposed to be at the point of death ; " † and that his ordination " was opposed by all the clergy, and many of the laity, as unlawful, because of his clinic perfusion." Gieseler, Ch. Hist. I. § 68. It was often necessary to baptize the sick, and in that case sprinkling was substituted for the usual rite.

\* Cyp. Epis. 76 (69) ad Magnum.
† Eccl. Hist. VI. 43. Valesius, in his note on this passage, says: " As baptism properly signifies immersion, *perfusion* could scarcely be called baptism." I take this note of Valesius from Dr. Sears (Christian Rev. III. 106), although admonished by his inaccurate citation of Eusebius, of the hazard of quoting at second hand. Hinton, Hist. Bap. p. 166.

Münscher. (Von Cöln) I. § 199. Only with the sick was baptism administered by aspersion; and it was deemed necessary to salvation, unless its place was supplied by the baptism of blood, i. e. martyrdom.

Fleury. Mœurs des Chrétiens, § 5, p. 192. Baptism was usually performed by immersion; yet aspersion was deemed sufficient in cases of necessity, as for the sick.

King. Prim. Ch. P. II, ch. 4, §§ 5, 6. Their usual custom was to immerse or dip the whole body. Perfusion, or sprinkling, was not accounted unlawful; but, in cases of necessity, that was used, as in clinic baptism.

To the same effect is the testimony of many other writers, who nevertheless practise sprinkling, Salmasius, Pamelius, Grotius, Rheinwald, Neander, Stroth, Du Fresne, Burnet, Towerson, Wall. It is worthy of remark that the same principle is now recognized in the Church of England, although the practice is very different, the Rubric requiring that the "priest dip the child, unless it be certified that it be weakly."

The primitive practice of immersion is so clearly sustained by ecclesiastical history, that it is conceded by every candid inquirer. The few among those who are not Baptists, who sometimes venture to deny it, are soon overwhelmed by the multitude of witnesses, that appear in their own ranks. Some of these will now be brought forward.

Dr. Wall. Their [the primitive Christians] general and ordinary way was to baptize by immersion, or dipping the person, whether it were an infant, or grown man or woman, into the water. This is so plain and clear by an infinite number of passages, that as one cannot but pity the weak endeavors of such pedobaptists as would maintain the negative of it; so also we ought to disown and show a dislike of the profane scoffs which some people give to the English anti-pedobaptists, merely for their use of dipping. It was, in all probability, the way by which our blessed Saviour, and for certain was the most usual and ordinary way by which the ancient Christians did receive their baptism.*

John Wesley. Mary Wesh, aged eleven days, was baptized according to the custom of the first

---

* Hist. Inf. Bap. II. ch. 2, p. 462. We may contrast with these sensible remarks, the *refinement* of some recent American writers. "It [immersion] is indelicate. It violates a natural and healthful sense of propriety for females to expose themselves in water, with and before the other sex. Though modesty forbids the statement of this objection in all its force, it is enough to say that the sacrifice of female modesty, in a religious rite, is an offering not required at our hands." Hints to an Inquirer. By Parsons Cooke and Joseph H. Towne. Boston: 1842. p. 59. The use of such an argument in support of affusion, presents an instance of what Cyprian might well denominate a "pressing necessity."

Church, and the rule of the Church of England, by immersion.*

Bossuet. We are able to make it appear, by the acts of councils, and by the ancient rituals, that for thirteen hundred years, baptism was thus administered throughout the whole Church, as far as possible.†

Von Cöln. Immersion in water was general until the thirteenth century; among the Latins it was then displaced by sprinkling, but retained by the Greeks.‡

Münscher. Baptism was generally performed by immersion. The baptism of the sick, which was performed by aspersion, is mentioned for the first time, in the third century. §

Usteri. The rite of baptism, by which the persons baptized were entirely immersed in water. Such is the testimony of the ancient witnesses. ‖

Klee, Roman Catholic Professor of Theology in the University at Bonn. Immersion was the mode of baptism ordinarily observed in the primitive age,

* Journal from his embarking for Georgia, p. 11.
† Stennett against Russen. p. 176.
‡ Dogmengesch. II. S. 203; also S. 208, where he cites the following passage from Thomas Aquinas. In immersione expressius repræsentatur figura sepulturæ Christi, et ideo hic modus baptizandi est communior et laudabilior. Summæ, P. III. Qu. 66. Art. 6.
§ Dogmengesch II. § 231.
‖ Paulin. Lehrbegr. S. 224.

in connection with which baptism by aspersion occurs as an exception to the rule.*

Prof. Stuart. "It is," says Augusti, "a thing made out," viz. the ancient practice of immersion. So indeed all the writers who have thoroughly investigated the subject. I know of no one usage of ancient times, which seems to be more clearly and certainly made out. I cannot see how it is possible for any candid man who examines the subject to deny this.†

Penny Cyclopædia. The manner in which it [baptism] was performed, appears to have been at first by complete immersion. John baptized in the Jordan; and in Enon, because there was much water there. The Ethiopian eunuch went down into the water to receive baptism from Philip. The words *baptism* and *to baptize* are Greek terms, which imply, in their ordinary acceptation, *washing*, or dipping. It was the practice of the English Church from the beginning, to immerse the whole body. ‡

Kitto's Cyclopedia of Biblical Literature. The whole body was immersed in water. §

---

\* Lehrb. der Dogmengesch. II. S. 147.
† Bibl. Repos. III. 359.
‡ Vol. III. 413, 414.
§ Art. Baptism. I. 288. See also Coleman's Christian Antiq. p. 275, and the citations in Christian Rev. III. 99 – 108. Hinton, Hist. Bap. 197 – 208. Booth, Pedobap. Exam. P. I. ch. 4.

The views which have been submitted, with reference to the nature of the external act of baptism, derive strong confirmation from the universal and invariable practice of the Greek Church. It is to be supposed that the members of that communion are acquainted with their own language; and therefore their mode of administering the rite of baptism affords a very satisfactory explanation of the meaning of the word. This has uniformly been immersion. Neudecker informs us, on the authority of the Orthodox Confession of the Greek church, Metrophanes, Critopulus, Stourdza, and others, that this is their present practice.* This church has always strenuously asserted the necessity of immersion to the validity of the ordinance; and has, in consequence, condemned and rejected the affusions of the Latin Church. An effort was made to unite the Oriental and Western Churches, at the session of the Council of Florence, A.D. 1439; and the Roman pontiff employed rewards, threats, and promises, to induce the Greeks to accede to his terms of accommodation. Mark of Ephesus, who was present at this council, maintained, in an encyclical letter addressed to all the Greek bishops and churches, the absolute impossibility of such a union, and that, too, upon the ground that the baptism

\* Munscher, Dogmengesch. ed. Neudecker, III. 618, where the requisite quotations are found.

# CHURCH POLITY. 167

of the Latins was an entirely different thing from that of the Greeks.*

It is a fatal objection to that perversion of the ordinance of baptism, which has become so common in western Christendom, that it is utterly destitute of support from apostolic or primitive practice, is at variance with the general practice of the Latins, for thirteen hundred years, and the uniform practice of the Greeks, down to the present day. Affusion was first tolerated in the third century, on the plea of necessity, a necessity founded on a most unscriptural and portentous error. This error, the alleged necessity of the rite to salvation, gave rise, as I shall presently show, to infant baptism; thus nullifying the ordinance, both in its mode and its subjects, and evincing the intimate connection which subsists between corruption in doctrine and error in practice.†

* Klee, Dogmengesch. II. 149. Mosheim, II. 502. Hague's Baptismal Question, p. 17. Coleman, Chr. Antiq. p. 266.

† The history of sprinkling is as curious as it is obscure. We have seen how pouring was introduced in the case of Novatian, and sustained by the authority of Cyprian († 258). The passage of Cyprian was introduced by Gratian into his Decretum (de Consecr. Dist. 4. cap. 126) A.D. 1150. Yet in the time of Thomas Aquinas († 1274), immersion was the more common practice, as we learn from the angelic doctor himself. He gives it as his judgment that although it is safer to baptize by immersion, because his was the more common, affusion or aspersion will answer the purpose, particularly in case of necessity. This

## II. SUBJECTS OF BAPTISM.

The genius of Christianity is peculiar. Recognizing no proxies or representatives between the sin-

necessity exists when, 1, there is a great multitude to be baptized; 2, water is scarce; 3, the administrator is feeble; 4, the candidate is feeble. A case occurred, under the first head, in the baptism of the Lithuanians, A.D. 1387. (It ought to be mentioned that the first ecclesiastical authority for sprinkling was given by the Council of Ravenna A.D. 1311. The case of Stephen, referred to by Hinton, p. 191, seems somewhat apocryphal. Basnagu Monumen. I. Præfat V. 4. Robin. Hist. Bap. 429). The circumstances were these: Jagello, Grand Duke of Lithuania, aspired to the hand of Hedwig, the heiress of the Polish crown; but neither she nor her subjects would favor his pretensions unless he became a good Catholic. Hence, although he had been baptized twice before, he consented to receive baptism again, in Cracow. Many of his subjects followed his example; and the Duke rewarded each of them, for this pious act, with a new suit of clothes. This was too great a temptation to the rest of the Lithuanians; they came in crowds to be baptized and get a new coat. Et quoniam labor immensus erat, &c., because the labor of baptizing such a multitude was too great, they were filed off into separate companies, and sprinkled, each company receiving a Christian name; as the company of Peter, of Paul, &c.; and every member of a particular company, bearing the name by which it was designated. Gieseler, Ch. Hist. § 124. Von Cöln, II. 209. The only persons who opposed immersion on any other ground except necessity, were Theophronius and Eutychius, the disciples of Eunomius, who poured water upon the head and arms. The reason which they gave for this practice is not fit to be repeated here. Vid. Klee, 11, 148.

ner and the Saviour, it urges its claims upon each individual of the race to whom it is sent, and its ultimate issues are suspended upon the personal reception or rejection of its gracious provisions. Salvation is found only in connection with the actual existence of the conditions which it demands in those upon whom the blessing is conferred. The commands of Christ must be obeyed in person, or not at all. That one individual should be baptized for another is absurd, as is universally conceded; but that one should perform for another the conditions on which alone the ordinance possesses any significance or value, although not so generally admitted, is equally opposed to the dictates of reason and conscience. The principle of substitution is, indeed, the grandest feature of the Christian scheme; but it relates solely to the vicarious work of the man Christ Jesus, the substitution of the innocent for the guilty; it does not affect the relations of the guilty among themselves. No moral being can do for another that which God requires at his own hands; and if repentance and faith are required of every individual to whom the message of the gospel comes, it is manifest that the existence of these graces in one can exert no direct influence upon another, nor change the relation in which he stands to God. Christianity, from its very nature, excludes all human mediators, proxies, or sponsors.

Such being the genius of the Christian revelation, if we proceed to examine the character of those upon whom its duties are imposed, we may justly expect to find in them those qualifications which define and constitute a moral agent. If any individuals of our race are destitute of these qualifications, we may fairly conclude that the gospel is not addressed to them. Infants and idiots are not moral agents; Christianity therefore demands nothing at their hands. They may, we believe they do, share in its benefits; but they do not come within the sphere of its requisitions. No Christian duty is enjoined upon them, for the obvious reason that they can perform none. The gospel does not require a natural and physical impossibility.

Baptism is a Christian duty, and is obligatory only on moral agents. Believers are the only proper subjects. This position is sustained:

1. By the evidence of the Scriptures.

The commission which imparts validity and force to this ordinance was given in the following words: "Go ye unto all the world, and preach the gospel to every creature. He that believeth and is baptized shall be saved, but he that believeth not shall be damned." Mark 16: 15, 16; cf. Matt. 28: 19. Here baptism is subsequent to faith, and is contemplated as the duty only of one that believeth. When this commission was given, the ordinance was already in existence and was familiar to the disciples. It is, therefore, relevant to revert to its previous history, to ascertain the meaning which they must have attached to the commission. Going back to "the beginning of the gospel of Jesus Christ," the baptism of John, we find that he preached repentance, and the people were baptized of him, "confessing their sins." Such is the testimony of Josephus, who affirms that John's baptism was administered on the supposition that "the soul was purified before by righteousness."* "Adult Jews," says Scott, in his comment on this passage of Mark, "were the only persons, so far as we can find, whom John admitted to baptism." We search the gospels in vain for any instance of infant baptism. Children were brought to Jesus. They were blessed, but not baptized; for it is expressly said that Jesus baptized not. John 4 : 2.

Such was the state of the case when the apostles received the commission. The practice of baptism was settled, so that even if that commission had been given in general terms — if it had embraced simply the command to baptize, they could have had no hesitation with respect to the subjects of baptism. But the commission is not general nor ambiguous; it is specific and plain. The direction to baptize is limited, in its application, to believers.

* Antiq. B. 18, c. 5, § 2.

The efforts which are made to evade the obvious import of the commission are more plausible than forcible. Thus it is alleged, by a writer who assumes that infant baptism was already in use in the time of the apostles, that "in giving directions, or issuing a command, certain things are always taken for granted as being well known, and we only aim to be explicit enough to be clearly understood. For instance, a messenger is sent to the post-office. The order issued is, 'go and bring my *papers*,' or simply, '*go to the post-office.*' The messenger goes and brings *letters*, *newspapers*, and *pamphlets*, and he *acts* in accordance with the *intention of him who sent him.*" * A command issued in terms so loose

---

* Infant Baptism, by Wm. Hodges, A.M., Phila., 1844, p. 168. The practice of proselyte baptism among the Jews in the age of the apostles, by which this writer, after Wall, proves the existence of infant baptism, cannot itself be proved. Dr. Gill assures us there is no mention made of it, either by the Jewish doctors or the Christian fathers of the first three or four centuries. Dissertation on Pros. Bap. Dr. Lardner considers it " a mere fiction of the Rabbins by whom we have suffered ourselves to be imposed upon." Letter to Dr. Doddridge. "It is at length settled by the great critics of Germany, that the existence of a proselyte baptism, as a Jewish institution in the time of Christ, cannot be proved." Christian Review, 3, p. 203. This is the judgment of such men as Neander, Olshausen, Hase, Böttiger, Winer, &c. But proselyte baptism, if admitted to have existed at that time, would be decidedly against the practice of pedobaptists. Children that were born *after* the parents' adoption of the Jewish religion, were *not* to be bap-

CHURCH POLITY. 173

as these may suit the case which has been suggested; but it could never find its way into any human statute, much less would it be incorporated in the great law of baptism, enacted by the Head of the Church, for all nations and for all times. The case is not a parallel one. To make it correspond with the commission, the order must be issued thus : — " Go and bring my letters ; those that are *post-paid* and *addressed to me*, bring ; those that are not *post-paid*, leave at the office." If the messenger were required not only to execute this commission, but to make it known for the benefit of his employer's correspondents, it would certainly be his duty to assure them that these terms are imperative, that a letter which was not *post-paid*, even if addressed to his employer, would not be received. Baptism is the ordinance by which an individual is *addressed* to Christ, indicated to be his ; but unless the other condition be fulfilled, unless faith be exercised, he will not be received. If the letter be not *post-paid* the address will not carry it to its destination. Whether some other arrangement may not have been made by his employer, by which those who *cannot* pay may secure the reception of their letters, is another question, which is not embraced in the terms of

tized. Analogy would require that the children of Christian parents should not be baptized; only the children who were born *before* the parents came to the rite would be entitled to participate in it.

his commission. So also, whether provision has been made for the salvation of those who cannot believe, is a distinct question, not dependent for its solution upon the commission of the Redeemer, with reference to the conditions of baptism. This explication affords a satisfactory reply to the argument which affirms that if, according to the commission, infants cannot be baptized, they cannot be saved. The commission has no reference to infants, and therefore does not determine the conditions of their salvation. It is addressed only to such as may be taught and may become disciples.

That the commission was so understood by the apostles is evident from their own subsequent practice. On the day of Pentecost Peter preached; many of his hearers were converted: "then they that gladly received the word were baptized, and the same day were added to them about three thousand souls. And they continued in the apostles' doctrine and fellowship," &c. Acts 2 : 41. Here the ordinance is restricted to those who "gladly received the word."

The next account of baptism occurs in Acts 8 : 12. "When they believed Philip, preaching the things concerning the kingdom of God, and the name of Jesus, they were baptized, both men and women." Nothing can be more expressive of the extent and limitation of the ordinance. The specific mention of men and women excludes the supposition that children were also baptized.

An argument in favor of infant baptism has been derived from the baptism of households. But it is founded upon the unwarrantable assumption that infants are necessarily included in a household. The baptism of entire households, upon a profession of faith, has become so common an occurrence that this argument has lost all its force. "There were eight baptized families belonging to the Karen Baptist Mission before it was as old as the apostolic mission, when the family of Lydia was baptized. The Christian Watchman of Jan. 29, 1841, presents authentic proof of the existence, at that time, of upwards of fifty baptized households, connected with Baptist churches—every member of whom was baptized on profession of faith, and added to the Church." * Such were probably the constituents of the households mentioned in the New Testament. Cornelius was "a devout man and one that feared God with all his house." Acts 10 : 2. Peter himself testifies that they had "received the Holy Ghost," before he "commanded them to be baptized." In Acts 18 : 8, we are informed : "Crispus the chief ruler of the synagogue believed on the Lord with all his house ; and many of the Corin-

* Crowell, Church Member's Manual. Boston, 1847. P. 158.

thians hearing, believed and were baptized." The household of Stephanus, baptized by Paul, "addicted themselves to the ministry of the saints," and could not therefore have been infants.

Even admitting that these households embraced infants, the fact proves nothing in favor of infant baptism. The apostles had no authority to baptize them, and therefore could not have done it. The nature of the case excludes them. It is required of a bishop that he be "one that ruleth well his own house." But this requisition cannot apply to newly-born infants, who are incapable of government. The nature of the case restricts it to adults, or at least to children who are old enough to be ruled. "There is," says Carson, "no axiom in mathematics more clear, than that the households are nothing to the purpose of infant baptism. If the term household does not necessarily imply infants, then there is no evidence from the term that there were infants in those households. Again, as such phraseology is, in daily conversation, used with exceptions, so, though infants had been in those households, the known limitations of the commission would exclude them." *

The fallacy of this argument has been fully exposed by a pedobaptist writer of great logical acumen, who candidly admits "that (historically con-

* Carson on Baptism, N. Y., 1832. P. 307.

sidered) there exists no sufficient *positive* evidence that the baptism of infants was instituted by the apostles, in the practice of the apostolic age. I have, I confess, no eye for these smoke-like wreaths of inference, this ever-widening spiral *ergo* from the narrow aperture of perhaps a single text; or rather an interpretation forced into it by construing an idiomatic phrase in an artless narrative with the same absoluteness as if it had formed part of a mathematical problem. I start back from these inverted pyramids, where the apex is the base. If I should inform any one that I had called at a friend's house, but had found nobody at home, the family having all gone to the play; and if he, on the strength of this information, should take occasion to asperse my friend's wife for unmotherly conduct, in taking an infant, six months old, to a crowded theatre, would you allow him to press on the words *nobody* and *all* the family, in justification of the slander? Would you not tell him that the words were to be interpreted by the nature of the subject, the purpose of the speaker, and their ordinary acceptation? and that he must or might have known that infants of that age would not be admitted into the theatre? Exactly so with regard to the words, 'he and all his household.' Had baptism of infants at that early period of the gospel been a known practice, or had this been previously demonstrated, then, indeed, the argument that in all probability there was one or more infants or young children in so large a family, would be no otherwise objectionable than as being superfluous, and a sort of anti-climax in logic. But if the words are cited as *the* proof, it would be a clear *petitio principii*, though there had been nothing else against it. But when we turn back to the Scriptures preceding the narrative, and find repentance and belief demanded as the terms and indispensable conditions of baptism—*then* the case above imagined applies in its full force. Equally vain is the pretended analogy from circumcision, which was no sacrament at all, but the means and mark of national distintcion." *

The scriptural argument in proof of our position is corroborated by the account which the apostles give of the meaning or spiritual design of baptism. "Know ye not that so many of us as were baptized into Christ were baptized into his death. Therefore we are buried with him by baptism, into death, that like as Christ was raised up from the dead by the glory of the Father, even so we also should walk in newness of life." Rom. 6 : 3. cf. Col. 2 : 12. Those who are baptized, are baptized into Christ's death, as dying with him, and as rising with him to a new life. Baptism is symbolical of a

* Coleridge, Aids to Reflection. Burlington, 1829. P. 220.

change, of which infants are incapable. Equally expressive is the language of Gal. 3 : 27. "For as many of you as have been baptized into Christ, have put on Christ." Here baptism implies a putting on of Christ, a fact which can be affirmed only of believers.

If the apostolic commission, the import of the rite, and the practice of the apostles clearly evince that baptism is to be administered only to those who profess faith in the Redeemer, no respect is due to the objections which have been urged against this position on the ground that certain passages in the New Testament imply the baptism of infants; such as Matt. 19 : 13 – 15\*; Acts 2 : 38, 39; 1 Cor. 7 : 12 – 14. All these passages are susceptible of an explanation which entirely accords with the baptism of believers.†

2. The testimony of ecclesiastical antiquity.

There exists no evidence in favor of the existence of infant baptism in the first century, but there is conclusive evidence against it. Justin Martyr, A.D. 140, thus describes the rite of baptism: "They who are persuaded and do believe that these things

---

\* Of this passage Carson remarks : "We might as well seek a warrant for infant baptism in Magna Charta, or the Bill of Rights. Baptism, p. 319.

† For a discussion of these points, the reader is referred to the works on Baptism. Carson, pp. 319—338. Hinton, Booth, and others.

which are taught by us are true, and do promise to live according to them, are directed first to pray, and ask of God, with fasting, the forgiveness of their former sins; and we also pray and fast together with them. Then we bring them to some place where there is water, and they are regenerated by the same way of regeneration by which we were regenerated; for they are washed with water in the name of God the Father and Lord of all things, and of our Saviour Jesus Christ, and of the Holy Ghost."*

There is another passage in Justin, which is pressed into the service of infant baptism. "There are many persons among us of both sexes, of sixty and seventy years of age, who were made disciples of Christ from their childhood."† But to employ the passage in this manner is not only to make the writer contradict the Scriptures, but contradict himself; for he has informed us, in the passage quoted above, that disciples are such as are "persuaded and do believe."

With just as little reason is the celebrated passage of Irenæus‡ alleged in support of this practice. It is too equivocal to constitute the basis of either argument or inference. Many of the most judicious

\* Justin Apol. I. Wall's Translation.
† Hodges on Infant Baptism, p. 112.
‡ Adv. Her. Lib. XI. c. 18.

and impartial critics, among pedobaptists, acknowledge that it affords no support for infant baptism.

Baumgarten Crusius says: "The celebrated passage in Irenæus, is not to be applied to infant baptism." *

The earliest allusion to the practice of infant baptism occurs in Tertullian, A.D. 200, and he opposes it.† A highly respectable writer in defence of infant baptism, has failed to appreciate the testimony of this Father, in consequence of following Wall, who himself confesses that he does not understand Tertullian.‡ "He had adopted," says this writer, "the strange notion that baptism washed away all *previous sin*, whether *actual* or *original*, and hence, the longer delayed, the better, when there appeared no immediate danger of death." This strange notion was by no means peculiar to Tertullian; and, moreover, it was not the point from which he argued against infant baptism. Had Dr. Wall, and those who have followed in his footsteps, studied the theo-

---

* Dogmengesch. S 1209. So also Engelhardt, Th. 1. S. 333. Münscher, 2, § 233.

† De Bap. 18. Robinson and Hinton, Hist. of Bap. p. 246, contend that there is no reference here to infant baptism; but their argument is founded upon an erroneous translation of the passage. They render *norint*, "they just know," instead of "let them know."

‡ Infant Baptism, &c. By William Hodges, A.M., Rector of Bruton Parish, Williamsburg, Va. Phila. 1844. pp. 87--93.

logical system of Tertullian, they would have been better able to appreciate his position on this subject. He had to contend with two opposite parties, the one holding that all persons, even infants, must be baptized in order to be saved, and the other, that baptism is not necessary at all, if one has sufficient faith. Against the former, he contends in the well-known passage referred to by Wall. His fundamental principle on the subject of baptism, as stated by himself, is: "Baptism is the seal of faith. We are not baptized *in order* to cease from sin, but because our hearts are already cleansed." * And he opposes infant baptism because it violates this principle, by placing baptism before faith. He, therefore, insists that the baptism of children should be delayed until they are old enough to "know Christ." He does not insist, as Wall and Mr. Hodges understood him, upon a mere delay of infant baptism, but on the postponement of baptism until the subjects of it should cease to be infants. But his opponents confronted him with the passage, "Suffer little children," &c. From this we learn that infant baptism was a subject of controversy; and yet that no tradition or divine command was pleaded by Tertullian's opponents. Indeed, it deserves particular notice, that in all the writings of Tertullian and Cyprian, both of whom treat of the subject as a

* De Poeniten, 6.

matter of controversy, *there is no allusion whatever* to an apostolical tradition in favor of the practice. Is it possible that these fathers of tradition could have overlooked so important a point? As Tertullian devised the method of meeting the heretics with the authority of tradition, would his opponents have spared him, if these weapons of his own could have been employed against him? His judicious reply to the passage of Scripture above quoted, was, "Let them come when they are grown up, — let them come when they understand and are taught whither they come, — let them become Christians, when they are capable of knowing Christ." He undoubtedly carried his caution too far in regard to virgins and widows; still the principle was a sound one, which required good evidence of piety before baptism.\*

3. The judgment of critics and historians.

In accordance with the principle which I have assumed as my guide in these inquiries, that the Scriptures constitute the only rule of faith and practice, it is pertinent to show that, even in the judgment of a large number of the abettors of infant baptism, it finds no support in the Word of God, and receives no countenance from the practice of those to whom the word of God was delivered, or of their immediate successors.

\* Christian Review, III. p. 214.

An eminent German writer, who has examined this subject with equal learning and candor, remarks: "Infant baptism was not yet customary in the first two centuries. The proofs which are alledged for its existence in the apostolic age, from the mention in Acts, of the baptism of whole families, and in the second century, from a passage in Irenæus, in which he speaks of the regeneration of children, are not satisfactory. Tertullian declared himself, most explicitly, against it, upon the ground that it imposed too heavy a responsibility upon the sponsors, and would be more beneficial to the children themselves, when they had arrived at an age in which they could know Christ, and appreciate the importance of baptism. In the time of Origen, however, infant baptism was already customary in the Church, at least, in the Egyptian portion of it, and was deemed an ordinance of the apostles. Origen vindicated its necessity on the same ground as that subsequently alledged by Augustine, viz.: that baptism was represented in the New Testament, as, in general, necessary to salvation; and, therefore, children ought to be baptized.\*

The celebrated philologist Koraes, one of the first Greek scholars of modern times, says: "Infant baptism seems to have been introduced in the third

---

\* Engelhardt. Dogmengeschichte. Th. 1. S. 333. Erlangen, 1839.

century; at first only in Africa, subsequently by degrees also in other countries. Not venturing to decide upon this matter we would only say, that even supposing infants to have been baptized in the apostolic times or shortly afterwards, the practice was neither uniformly adopted, nor always nor everywhere observed. This is evident from numerous instances of persons living in or about the fourth century, who were not baptized until after they had reached the age of manhood. Such was the case with Ambrose, Jerome, Augustine, Chrysostom, Basil, Gregory; and among the emperors with Constantine, Constantius, Valentinian, Gratian, Theodosius, and with innumerable other persons. The discourses addressed by many of the Fathers of the same century to persons deferring baptism, prove the same thing. It is further confirmed by the canons of several councils, and also by the well-known anecdote of Athanasius the Great, who, when a boy, on a certain occasion whilst at play, catechised and baptized his play-fellows, who, until then, had remained unbaptized. The time when infant baptism was generally introduced cannot easily be determined."*

\* Leslie's Hist. View of the Baptists, p. 33. Here we have the children of Christian parents remaining unbaptized. The first instance on record of the baptism of a child, is that of Galates, the dying son of the Arian empe-

"All the earlier traces of infant baptism are very doubtful. Tertullian is the first who refers to it; and he censures it. Origen and Cyprian, on the contrary, defend it. In the fourth century its validity was generally acknowledged, although the church Fathers often found it necessary to warn against the delay of baptism. Even Pelagius did not dare to call the correctness of it in question. Augustine pointed out the removal of original sin, and the sins of the children, as its definite object; and through his representations was its universal diffusion promoted."*

"As baptism signified an entrance into fellowship with Christ, it readily followed from the nature of the case, that a profession of faith in Jesus as the Redeemer, should be made by the candidate at the time. Since baptism was thus immediately connected with a conscious and voluntary accession to the Christian fellowship, and faith and baptism were always united, it is highly probable that the custom of infant baptism was not practised in this age. From the example of the baptism of whole families we can by no means infer the existence of infant baptism. One passage, 1 Cor. 16 : 15, shows the

---

ror Valens, who was baptized by order of the monarch, who swore that he would not be contradicted. Christian Review, p. 6, May, 1846.

* Munscher (Ed. Von Cöln) Dogmengesch. I. S. 469.

incorrectness of such an inference; for it thence appears that the whole family of Stephanus, who all received baptism from Paul, was composed of adult members."*

" Commands or plain and certain examples, in the New Testament, relating to it, I do not find."†

" There is no express command for infant baptism found in the New Testament."‡

If infant baptism be thus destitute of support in the word of God, an inquiry naturally arises as to its origin, and the reasons for its introduction. To this the observations of a learned living historian furnish a satisfactory reply. "The first public recognition of infant baptism was A. D. 250. It may be supposed to have existed anterior to that period, and to have been gradually working its way into the church, along with other corruptions. But the grand error, under sanction of which it obtained prevalence, was that baptism and regeneration was one and the same thing. So soon as that came to be a general belief, it was deemed necessary, in order

---

* Neander, in Bibl. Repos. IV. p. 272.
† Prof. Stuart, Bibl. Repos. III, p. 385.
‡ Knapp. Theology, II. p. 535. Storr and Flatt speak of the silence of the N. T. concerning it. Bibl. Theol. p. 527. See also, Gieseler, Church Hist. I, pp. 93, 98, 195. Mosheim, I. p. 167. Booth has collected a host of similar witnesses, in his Pedobaptism Examined. Part II, ch. I.

to insure the spiritual illumination of infants, to have them baptized."*

It thus appears that the changes which have been introduced since the age of the Apostles, with reference both to the subjects and the mode of baptism, were founded upon a portentous error, the identity of baptism and regeneration, and, therefore, the necessity of the rite to salvation. In immediate connection with this, we find another error of equal magnitude. The great patron of affusion and infant baptism, Cyprian, furnishes the first distinct allusion to a practice, the existence of which would scarcely be deemed credible, were it not most amply attested, the communion of infants at the Lord's supper. This practice was coëxtensive with infant baptism, and rested upon the same grounds, the necessity of the rite to salvation. "It was common in Africa in Cyprian's time, i. e. in the third century, to give the sacramental elements even to children; and this custom was gradually introduced into other churches. But in the twelfth century this practice fell into disuse in the West;

---

* Neander, Hist. Chr. Religion, p. 361. So, also, Meier, Dogmengesch, S. 132. Giessen, 1840. Mosheim, I, p. 230. Gieseler, I, p. 159, note 4. "If we except Tertullian," says Wall, "Vincentius (A, D. 419) is the first man upon record that ever said that children might be saved without baptism." Booth, Pedobap. Exam. P. II, ch. 3, § 8,

although in the East it continues to the present day,"*

Infant baptism and infant communion rest on the same foundation, the authority of the Fathers of the third century.

III. Efficacy of baptism.

On this point, professors of Christianity are divided into three great parties, the first of which regards baptism as an act of obedience to Christ, and a symbol, or sign of certain truths implied in the ordinance; the second, as a seal or pledge of spiritual blessings; while the third exalts it to the dignity of an efficacious instrument of grace, some ascribing to it a physical, and others only a hyperphysical, or moral efficacy.† Of these various theories, the second and third are unscriptural, and besides, are encumbered with other serious objections; so that an elucidation of the grounds upon which the first is sustained, will furnish their appropriate refutation.

The Scriptures no where ascribe to baptism any

---

\* Knapp, Theology, II. p. 555. Mosheim, I. p. 230. § 3, note. Gieseler, I. p. 159. Münscher (Ed. Von Cöln), I. S. 481. Meir, § 68. S. 163. Hinton, Hist. Bap. pp. 323-330. Chillingworth, Works, p. 744. Phila. 1841.

† Turrettini Op. Loc. XVIII. Quæst. 8. Münscher, (Ed. Neudecker) III. S. 601--628. Hinton, Hist. Bap. chap. X. "Baptism is the divinely appointed form of ratifying God's covenant of grace with every believer ... and is in its nature a pledge, on his part, of spiritual blessings," &c. Crowell, Ch. Mem. Manual, p. 152.

peculiar efficacy, physical or moral, essential or accidental. It is simply the appointed method of professing faith in the Redeemer; and if, in some places, a preëminence is given to it over other acts of obedience, it is because it is the first of a series which are incumbent on the believer. "That baptism and the Lord's Supper are seals of the covenant, is a doctrine so common, and a phraseology so established, that it is received without question as a first principle. They who measure truth by the attainments of our ancestors, look upon the questioning of this dogma as a kind of impiety and heresy; and even the modern Independents, who have professed to be guided solely by the Bible, have very generally continued to speak in the same language. While I highly respect and value the ancient writers who speak in this manner, I strongly protest against it as unscriptural, and as laying a foundation for receiving other things on the authority of man. Is there any Jewish tradition more void of scriptural authority, than that which designates baptism and the Lord's Supper *seals of the New Covenant?* There is not in the New Testament any single portion that can bear such a meaning. And what can the wisest of men know about these things, but what God has told us? He has not said that baptism is a seal. Circumcision was a seal of the righteousness of the faith of Abraham. This was God's seal to that truth, till the letter was abolished. The spirit of the truth is the seal, and the circumcision of the heart by him, is the thing signified by circumcision in the flesh. The circumcised nation was typical of the Church of Christ; for the apostle says "we are the circumcision which worship God in the spirit;" and "circumcision is that of the heart, in the spirit, and not in the letter." The circumcision of the Jews was the letter, of which the circumcision of the heart in Christians is the spirit. The Christian, then, has a more exalted seal than circumcision. He has the Spirit of God, "whereby he is sealed unto the day of redemption." Eph. 4: 30. When sinners believe in Christ, they are sealed with the Holy Spirit of promise, which is the "earnest of their inheritance until the redemption of the purchased possession." Eph. 1: 13. The seal, then, that comes in the room of circumcision, is the seal of the Spirit. When the Holy Spirit himself, in the heart of the believer, is the seal of God's truth, there is no need of any other seal. Baptism represents the belief of the truth in a figure, and takes it for granted that they are believers to whom it is applied; but it is no seal of this. They may appear to be Christians to-day, and therefore ought to be baptized; to-morrow they may prove the contrary, and therefore they cannot have been sealed by baptism. He that is once sealed by the Spirit, is secured to eternity." *

This theory, although unscriptural, is, except in its application to infant baptism, comparatively harmless, since it supposes the existence of such spiritual qualifications in the baptized, as are connected with the enjoyment of spiritual blessings. But the third theory is open to more serious objections; for, although various representations of it are given by its different advocates, it involves, as its distinctive principle, the assumption that baptism sustains a direct relation to the germination and growth of the divine life in the soul; and is, therefore, in general, necessary to salvation. Whether this ordinance be described as the laver of regeneration, the bath in which original sin is washed away, or the medium through which forgiveness of sin, and the influences of the Spirit are imparted, the radical idea of the theory is the same. It makes the acceptance of a sinner with God, in some way dependent upon his reception of baptism. But if the Scriptures furnish us with such a statement of the ground of a sinner's acceptance as excludes baptism, as well as all other works, the entire theory is false. That this is the case, I shall endeavor to show.

* Carson, on Baptism, pp. 375-377. Georgia Pulpit, p. 142.

With respect to the plan of salvation, the Scriptures are sufficiently explicit. They teach that the ground of a sinner's acceptance with God, is not any thing done by him, or in him, but is the perfect work of the Lord Jesus Christ. As the substitute of guilty man, he has met all the claims of the divine government against him, has obeyed the law, and suffered its penalty; and has thus brought in an everlasting righteousness, which is imputed to the believer for justification. As soon as a sinner truly believes, he is justified, accepted, and his final salvation secured. Faith sustains this peculiar relation to justification, that it appropriates Him who is our righteousness. It is, therefore, essential to our acceptance with God; but nothing else is. To make baptism thus essential, which is not the act by which we trust in Christ, but simply an act of obedience rendered by one already justified, is to confound the consequent with the antecedent; to mistake the symbolical expression of a believer's love to Christ on account of the remission of sin — a love which manifests itself effectually by keeping his commandments — for the medium through which that remission is conferred.

That this is the teaching of the Scriptures on this subject, is evinced by the following, among many passages: "He that believeth hath everlasting life." John 5: 24; 3: 16, 36. "With the heart man believeth unto righteousness." Rom. 10 : 10. "By grace are ye saved through faith." Eph. 2 : 8. "Being justified by faith, we have peace with God, through our Lord Jesus Christ." Rom. 5 : 1. "They which are of faith, the same are the children of Abraham." Gal. 3 : 7. "The blood of Jesus Christ his Son cleanseth us from all sin." 1 John 1 : 8. "Ye are all the children of God by faith in Jesus Christ." Gal. 3 : 26. cf. John 5 : 24; Acts 13 : 39; Rom. 3 : 21, 22, 25, 26; 4 : 5; 10 : 4; Phil, 3 : 8–10; John 1 : 12; Acts 10 : 42; John 3 : 14–18, 40; 20 : 31; Rom. 10 : 9.

The case of the Philippian jailer is decisive on this point. His inquiry had distinct reference to the plan of salvation. He came, a convicted sinner, to Paul and Silas, and sought direction. "Sirs, what must I do to be saved?" Had they omitted in their reply anything essential, they would have misled the inquiring jailer. The circumstances of the case demanded that they should comprehend in their instructions all that was necessary to salvation. But they simply say: "Believe on the Lord Jesus Christ, and thou shalt be saved, and thy house." Acts 16 : 31. The absence of any reference to baptism here shows that, in the judgment of the apostles, it has no reference to that primary act of faith, by which a penitent obtains the forgiveness of sin.

From these considerations, and others which will be adduced, it is evident that the theory which suspends the remission of sin upon the reception of baptism, is contrary to the first principle of the Gospel of Christ.

Another fatal objection to this theory, is found in the fact that cases occur, in the New Testament, of persons who received the assurance of forgiveness prior to baptism. Among these, are the woman who was a sinner, the sick of the palsy, and the dying malefactor.* Moreover, it is contradicted by Christian experience. Every converted man knows that the assurance of forgiveness is obtained by faith in Christ. Thousands of such have been brought to the knowledge of the truth, have rejoiced in God through our Lord Jesus Christ, and afterwards put on Christ in baptism, not to obtain remission of sin, but because they had already been assured of possessing that blessing, and without which they would not have ventured to approach the emblematic grave. They were conscious of being constrained to do this by love to the Redeemer; and they rejoiced in the consolation that "every one that loveth is born of God and knoweth God," and "whosoever

---

* Luke 7: 37--48.   Matt. 9: 2.   Luke 23: 39--43.

is born of God overcometh the world."* In addition to this it is worthy of remark, that a large portion of the most conscientious and devoted servants of God, in every part of the world, are, in the judgment of some of the most strenuous advocates of this theory, yet unbaptized, and, therefore, must remain unpardoned. They are yet in their sins. They have no hope in Christ, no assurance of acceptance with God, and dying in this state, they must encounter his wrath in the world to come. A theory which involves such shocking sentiments, as its legitimate consequences, which comes so directly in conflict with Christian consciousness, must be a false and unwarrantable assumption.

If any thing further were neccessary to expose the falsity of this theory, we might refer to Paul's view of the relative importance of baptism. As a preacher of the Gospel, he exulted in his mission; for the gospel is the power of God to salvation, to every one that believeth. Rom. 1: 16. In 1 Cor. 1: 17, he says: "Christ sent me not to baptize, but to preach the gospel." But in Acts 26: 17, 18, he affirms that "Christ sent him to the Gentiles, to turn them from darkness to light, and from the power of Satan unto God;" in other words, to accomplish their salvation. If baptism sustains the relation to salvation which is ascribed to it by this

* 1 John 4: 7; 5: 4.

theory, the manner in which the apostle underrates it, is utterly unaccountable. If the ordinance were indispensable, in general, to secure remission of sin, he could not have affirmed that Christ sent him not to baptize; for upon that supposition the preaching of the gospel, without baptism, would be a nullity. It would fail to accomplish the great end for which the Son of God was exalted as a Prince and a Saviour. Acts 5: 31.

Although this theory is thus subversive of the terms of acceptance with God, and opposed to Christian consciousness, its abettors labor to sustain it from the word of God, referring to several passages in its support. Before examining them, it may be well to make the general remark, that if they inculcated the error in question, the interpreter would find it impossible to reconcile them with other portions, as well as with the general tenor of the Scriptures. Unless, therefore, he would place divine truth in conflict with itself, he must resort to some other interpretation of these passages. It would be better to leave them unexplained than to elicit from them a sentiment so essentially at war with the whole Christian system. But these passages, so far from presenting any real difficulty, are susceptible, most easily and naturally, of an interpretation which keeps them in harmony with the doctrine of the apostles.

These passages will now be adduced.

Mark 16 : 16. He that believeth and is baptized shall be saved; but he that believeth not shall be damned.

The nature of these restrictions will be sufficiently clear, if we consider that faith, implying of course regeneration, is the first development of spiritual life in the soul, and baptism is its first outward manifestation. As soon as a sinner believes, he is to confess Christ in this ordinance. This is his first act of obedience. It is therefore perfectly natural that baptism should be selected from the various Christian duties, as the representative of the whole. The meaning of the passage, therefore, is, he that believes and acts accordingly — who possesses that genuine faith which works by love, and purifies the heart — shall be saved. The language of the commission, when properly explained, attaches no more importance to baptism than to any other Christian duty. It is the spirit of obedience which it demands; and baptism is indicated as the expression of that spirit, because it stands first in the series of Christian duties. In perfect accordance with these sentiments is the teaching of Paul, in Rom. 10: 10. "If thou shalt confess with thy mouth the Lord Jesus, and shalt believe in thine heart that God hath raised him from the dead, thou shalt be saved. For with the heart man believeth unto righteousness [justification], and with the mouth confession is made unto salvation." The apostle in this portion of the epistle contrasts the method of justification on which the Jews insisted, which was legal, and, when properly understood, perfectly impracticable, with the gospel method of salvation, which prescribes no such severe terms, but simply requires cordial faith and open profession. Confession is the fruit and external evidence of faith, assuring us of its vitality and power, as wrought by the Spirit of God. "No man can say that Jesus is the Lord but by the Holy Ghost." 1 Cor. 12: 3. "Whosoever shall confess that Jesus is the Son of God, God dwelleth in him and he in God." 1 John, 4: 15. Hence the necessity of a public confession of Christ unto salvation is asserted in the Scriptures. Matt. 10: 32. Luke, 12: 8. It is certain that he who deliberately refuses to confess Christ will be lost, because this refusal proves that he possesses no genuine faith; but this confession may be made fully and clearly prior to baptism, and, as in the case of dying penitents, without the intervention of baptism at all. "Though faith and confession are both necessary" observes an able expositor, "they are not necessary on the same grounds, nor to the same degree. The former is necessary as a means to an end, as without faith we can have no part in the justifying righteousness of Christ; the latter as a duty, the performance of which circumstances may render impracticable. In like manner Christ declares baptism, as the appointed means of confession, to be necessary; not however as a *sine qua non*, but as a command, the obligation of which providential dispensations may remove; as in the case of the thief on the cross."*

John 3: 5. Except a man be born of water and of the Spirit, he cannot enter into the kingdom of God.

Nothing but an invincible necessity would authorize such an interpretation of this passage as would elicit from it the doctrine of baptismal regeneration. This necessity does not exist. Many of the most learned and judicious commentators interpret the expression *water and the spirit*, by hendiadis, spiritual water. This mode of expression is common in the New Testament. Comp. Matt. 4: 16. In the region and shadow of death, i. e. the region of the shadow of death. 1 Cor. 2: 4. In the demonstration of the powerful spirit. Col. 2: 8. Acts, 17: 25.† This interpretation is confirmed by the fact that our Lord, in contrasting spiritual with natural regeneration, in the next verse, does not mention water at all, but merely opposes the

---

\* Hodge on Romans, p. 436.
† Grotius in loco. Calvin, Winer, Teller. See also Dr. Dagg's detailed examination of the passage, Phila. 1839.

spirit to the flesh, as the original principles of these different kinds of birth. If, however, Christ be supposed to refer to baptism, it must be under the same restrictions that are found in the apostolic commission, which has already been explained.

Acts, 2 : 38. Repent and be baptized every one of you for the remission of sins, [or, literally, unto the remission.]

This clause is easily understood by comparing it with others of similar construction. John says, in Matt. 3 : 11, "I baptize you with water unto repentance." He did not mean that repentance was procured, but was professed, in baptism; for he demanded of those who approached the baptismal stream "fruits meet for repentance," the evidence that they had already repented. But Peter has given us his own views, in Acts 3 : 19. "Repent ye therefore and be converted, that your sins may be blotted out," &c. If baptism is as inseparable from forgiveness as repentance is, the apostle is guilty of an unpardonable omission. If he has made no omission, but has stated fully the conditions of pardon, the dogma in question receives no support from his authority.

Acts 22 : 16. Arise and be baptized and wash away thy sins, calling upon the name of the Lord.

As baptism is symbolical of the purification of the soul, it is perfectly natural, because in accordance with a very common mode of speech, that the symbol should be put for the reality. Paul may be said to have washed away his sins in baptism, because in that sacred rite he made a public declaration of the fact. If this passage stood alone, it might occasion some difficulty, but taken in connection with the uniform teaching of the word of God, which suspends forgiveness of sin upon the exercise of faith in the Redeemer, it affords no countenance to the dogma of baptismal regeneration.*

\* For the various forms in which this dogma is held, the reader is referred to Hinton on Baptism, chap. 8. 10; Howell on Communion, chap. XII.; Ferdinand Walter, Lehrbuch des Kirchenrechts (Bonn. 1839), § 274, Landis' Review of Cambellism, in Biblical Repository (new series), vol 1, together with Mr. Campbell's reply, in the same work. Baptist Preacher, vol. 2, sermon by Rev. J. B. Jeter. The Confessions of Faith of the various denominations. The view of the Baptists is thus set forth in the Baptist Catechism: Charleston, S. C., 1813, a work originally published by the Baptists of Great Britain, A.D. 1689, and adopted by the Philadelphia Association, in 1742, "Quest. 97. What is Baptism? Ans. Baptism is an ordinance of the New Testament, instituted by Jesus Christ, to be unto the party baptized a sign of his fellowship with him, in his death, and burial, and resurrection, of his being ingrafted into him, of remission of sins, and of his giving himself up unto God, through Jesus Christ, to live and walk in newness of life."

# CHAPTER XV.

### THE LORD'S SUPPER.

Our blessed Lord, on the night preceding his crucifixion, instituted a solemn memorial of his death, to be religiously observed by his followers, until the end of time. To this the apostle refers in the following words: "I have received of the Lord that which I also delivered unto you, that the Lord Jesus, the same night in which he was betrayed, took bread: And when he had given thanks, he brake it, and said, Take, eat, this is my body, which is broken for you : this do in remembrance of me. After the same manner also he took the cup, when he had supped, saying, This cup is the New Testament in my blood : this do ye, as oft as ye drink it, in remembrance of me. For as often as ye eat this bread, and drink this cup, ye do shew the Lord's death till he come." * The nature and the perpetuity of this ordinance are here expressly declared ; and as the apostles were instructed to teach the churches to observe all things whatsoever Christ had commanded them,† the death of the

\* 1 Cor. 11 : 23--26; cf. Matt, 26, Luke 21, Mark 15.
† Matt 28 : 20.

Redeemer was universally commemorated among them in this manner.

The titles by which this service is known in the Scriptures are these: the Lord's Supper, the Lord's Table, the Communion of the Body and Blood of Christ, the New Testament in his Blood, the Breaking of Bread, and the Eucharist. Ecclesiastical writers have referred to it, under other appellations, as the sacrament, the mass; but these are not to be found in the word of God.*

1. The nature and design of the ordinance.

It is simply commemorative, and might be styled a symbolical sermon on the death of the Redeemer. "The Lord's Supper was not appointed to be a test of brotherly love among the people of God. It was intended to teach and exhibit the most interesting of all truths, and the most wonderful of all transactions. The design of the great institutor was, that it should be a memorial of God's love to us, and of Immanuel's death for us; that, the most astonishing favor ever displayed; this, the most stupendous fact that angels ever beheld."† The erroneous notion that this ordinance furnishes a test of Christian fellowship, is founded on a misinterpretation of the lan-

---

* Picteti Theologia Christiana, Lib. XIV., cap. 5. Turrettini Theol. Elenc., Loc. XIX. Quæst. 21. Opera. III. p. 359. New York, 1847.

† Booth, Vindication, sec. 1. Howell on Communion, p. 105, Phila. A. B. P, S. 1847.

guage of Paul, 1 Cor. 10 : 16. "The cup of blessing which we bless, is it not the communion of the blood of Christ? The bread which we break, is it not the communion of the body of Christ?" The apostle is here urging his brethren to "flee from idolatry;" and his argument is as follows: He who partakes of the elements of the Lord's Supper, indicates, by that act, his communion or connexion with Christ: so also, he who eats of the sacrifices offered to idols, places himself in communion with idols. The two things are therefore inconsistent. "I would not that ye should have fellowship with devils. Ye cannot drink the cup of the Lord, and the cup of devils: ye cannot be partakers of the Lord's table, and of the table of devils." The passage refers to fellowship with Christ, and not with each other, and furnishes additional proof that the design of the ordinance is to "shew the Lord's death." *

It is one of the enormous figments of Popery, that, in the Lord's Supper, "Christ is truly present, and indeed in such a way, that Almighty God, who was pleased at Cana, in Galilee, to convert water into wine, changes the inward substance of the consecrated bread and wine into the body and blood of

---

* This was the view of the older Baptists. See the Baptist Catechism (London, 1689), Quest. 102.

Christ." * This is the doctrine of transubstantiation. Its gross absurdity is manifest both from reason and from Scripture. It is contradicted by the clear and undisputable testimony of our senses, which affirm that no change has occurred in the nature and properties of the bread and wine. Confidence in the evidence of the senses is a law of our nature. If it is to be rejected, the Bible must be rejected with it, for our belief of the Scriptures rests upon the evidence of the senses.† This dogma is opposed to the universal observation of mankind, that all bodies (material substances,) must occupy definite portions of space, and cannot be in more than one place at the same time; for according to this tenet, every portion of consecrated bread is really the whole material body of the Saviour. His body is therefore present in Heaven and in many different places on the earth, at the same moment. Again, the bread and wine, after they are consecrated, are subject to decomposition, which would not be the case if they were transmuted into the glorified body of the Redeemer. They remain, what the apostle calls them, even after their consecration, bread and wine.‡

* Möhler, Symbolism, p. 311.

† 1 Jno. 1 : 3; Jno. 3 : 11; Luke 24 : 29.

‡ 1 Cor. 10 : 16; 11 : 26. Carson on Transubstantiation, Protestant Quarterly Review. I. p. 137--178, a most masterly argument. Storr and Flatt, Bibl. Theol. p. 545.

So far as this monstrous dogma pretends to any support from the Scriptures, it rests upon the literal interpretation of expressions which are manifestly figurative. The words, "this is my body," are supposed to affirm the actual presence of Christ's body in the elements of the eucharist. But Christ also says, "I am the vine, the way, the door," &c. When, therefore, he affirms of the bread, "this is my body," we have his own authority for understanding him to teach us that the bread is the sign or symbol of his body. No maxim of common sense is more plain, than that language must be interpreted figuratively, whenever a literal interpretation would teach an absurdity. This principle is recognized by the heathen in a case parallel with this. "When," says Cicero, "we call fruits, Ceres, and wine, Bacchus, we employ the language of common life; for who is so stupid as to suppose that what he eats is God?"* It was, also, applied to the interpretation of this expression of our Lord by the earliest Fathers. †

Upon this sandy foundation the papacy rears its portentous doctrine of the sacrifice of the mass for the living and the dead, by which Christ is dishonored and the Man of Sin exalted; a doctrine which

\* Nat. Deor, III. 16.
† Tertullian, Lib. IV. contra Marc. Hoc est corpus meum id est figura corporis mei. August. Epist. ad Adimant. cap. 12, signum daret corporis sui. Vid Picteti Theol. Lib. XIV. cap. 6, 7.

contradicts the testimony of the earliest and purest witnesses to the truth, and totally subverts the glorious gospel of the blessed God.*

In consequence of the exaggerated notion of the holiness of the consecrated elements, transmuted as they were into the real body, blood, and divinity of the Lord, the practice was introduced of withholding the cup from the laity, and thus mutilating the ordinance, contrary to the divine command: "Drink ye *all*, of it." With respect to the perpetrators of this impious assault upon an institution of Christ, it is said, by a sophistical advocate of Rome: "A pious dread of desecrating by spilling and the like, even in the most conscientious ministration, the form of the sublimest and the holiest, whereof the participation can be vouchsafed to man, was the feeling which swayed their minds." † Upon such slight pretences do men venture to annul a divine statute.

The Scriptural doctrine on this subject is, that "worthy receivers outwardly partaking of the visible

---

* For the history of Transubstantiation and its affiliated errors, which are of comparatively recent origin, vide Munscher Dogmengeschichte. (Ed. Von Cöln, §§ 103, 104, 142—145. Knapp, Theol. II. § 146). The Protestant's Evidence, by Simon Birckbek, p. 37. London, 1635. Dowling, Hist. Romanism, pp. 192, etc. Gibbon, Rom. Emp. IV. p. 160, who says: "Innocent III. may boast of the two most signal triumphs over sense and reason: the establishment of transubstantiation, and the origin of the inquisition"

† Möhler, Symbolism, p. 322.

elements in this ordinance, do then also inwardly by faith, really and indeed, yet not carnally and corporally, but spiritually, receive and feed upon Christ crucified, and all the benefits of his death: the body and blood of Christ being then not corporally or carnally, but spiritually present to the faith of believers in that ordinance, as the elements themselves are to the outward senses."*

2. The communicants.

The Lord's Supper is a social ordinance, and is celebrated by a church in its distinctive character, as a body of baptized believers. Whatever, therefore, determines the conditions of membership, defines also the terms of communion. That baptism is prior to the supper, in the order of their observance, and, therefore, that only the baptized have a right to commune, is so unquestionably the teaching of the Word of God, and was so manifestly the practice of the primitive churches, that we are not surprised at the almost universal agreement of Christians on this point. The splendor of a great name may, for a time, give prominence to the opposite error, which inverts the order of the rites; and a spurious charity may plead for its adoption; but the subject is too plain to admit of much diversity of sentiment or practice. It has, indeed, scarcely ever been deemed worthy of a labored discussion. All

* Baptist Confession of Faith, Chap. XXXI. § 7

the professed followers of the Redeemer, in all ages, with the exception of a very small minority, have concurred in the opinion that the Scriptures make Baptism an indispensable prerequisite to the Lord's Supper.*

Amid this universal agreement, with reference to the principle of communion, there could have been no diversity in practice, had all Christians concurred, to the same extent, in regard to the ordinance of baptism. It is at this point that they diverge. Had there remained one baptism, as well as one Lord, and one faith, there would have been but one communion. From this point of view, it is easy for a candid mind to understand the real nature of the difference between Baptists and other denominations, with reference to the Lord's table. The former hold that nothing but the immersion of a believer is baptism; but as they maintain, in common with other denominations, that baptism must precede communion, they cannot receive any one who has not been immersed. It is perfectly clear, therefore, that the only question at issue between them and the others, is as to what constitutes baptism. To represent the matter otherwise, for the purpose of arraying prejudices against them, and enlisting the passions where reason fails, is ungenerous as well as

---

* Booth, Vindic. Bap. Sec. 1. Remington, Def. of Restricted Communion. King, Prim. Ch P. II. ch. vi.

unfair. Yet upon no point have the Baptists been so frequently assailed or so generally misrepresented. To receive unimmersed persons to their communion, would amount not only to a virtual renunciation of their own views of baptism, but an abandonment of the fundamental law of communion, in the churches of Christ in general. And yet, because they refuse to do this, the cry of bigotry is raised against them. It would be well for those who are disposed to join in this cry, to consider what respect they could have for persons who would thus betray, at once, their own principles and the common principles of the Christian world.*

* For a more full discussion of this topic, the reader is referred to Dr. Howe l's work on Communion. Phila., A. B. P. Society. 1847

## CHAPTER XVI.

### RELATION OF CHURCHES TO EACH OTHER.

ALTHOUGH the churches of Jesus Christ are independent bodies, yet as they are constituted on the same principles, acknowledging one Lord, one faith, one baptism, and aim at the same great end, the spread of the Redeemer's kingdom, it is their duty to maintain friendly intercourse and fellowship with each other, for the promotion of their mutual interests and their common welfare. In visible organization they are many; but in spirit, in doctrine, in design, they are one.*

This friendly relation is evinced by admitting one another's members to transient communion, dismissing and receiving members to and from each other, and by affording assistance and giving advice in cases of difficulty or need. One church may send spiritual teachers to another. Such were sent by the church in Jerusalem to the church in Antioch.† They may supply each other's temporal necessities.‡ In cases

\* 1 Cor. 12 : 13; Eph. 4 : 5; 6 : 18; Jno. 17: 20—26; Rom. 16 : 1, 2 ; 3 Jno. 8—10 ; Acts 15.

† Acts 11 : 22—27; 15 : 22—27; 18 : 27; Eph. 6 : 21; 1 Cor. 16 : 15—18.

‡ 1 Cor. 16: 1—3; 2 Cor. 8 : 1—4, 13—24 ; 9 : 1—15; Rom. 15 : 26.

of perplexity menacing their peace or purity, they may avail themselves of the services of their brethren, by seeking the advice of presbyteries or councils, composed of the pastors and delegated members of sister churches. " A council has no power whatever but to examine, and give its opinion and advice. It can exercise no control. Its office is to give light, not to pronounce decrees." \* The decision of the case, whatever it may be, must rest upon the final determination of the church.

Some of the objects contemplated in the institution of Christian churches, can be best secured by their coöperation; as the general spread of the gospel, the gathering of new churches, the education of the ministry, and the circulation of the Scriptures, and other religious books. This principle was recognized by the apostles, and the churches which they founded. The church in Antioch sent forth Paul and Barnabas on a missionary excursion, and other churches cordially aided in their support.† To accomplish these objects, churches, at the present day, unite in Associations, and through them, in a general Convention.

An association consists of delegates or messengers from different particular churches. As the union of the members of a particular church is founded on

---

\* Bacon's Manual, p. 145.
† Acts 13 : 2, 3; 2 Cor. 11 : 8, 12 : 13, 18; Phil. 6 : 10 – 18.

uniformity of faith and practice, so the union of churches in a general body rests upon the same principles. Thus constituted, an association is not armed with coercive powers. Its authority is representative, executive, advisory. To execute the wishes of the churches, in reference to the objects for which it was organized, and to offer its advice, in cases which involve the common interest of the confederation, are all that it may lawfully do. Should any of the churches included in the association depart from the principles of the union, by embracing error, abusing its power over its members, or neglecting attendance on the meetings of the association, it is the right and duty of this body to remonstrate, to advise, and if the church proves incorrigible, to withdraw fellowship from it; "for if the agreement of several distinct churches in sound doctrine and regular practice, be the binding motive, ground, foundation, or basis of their confederation, then it must naturally follow, that a defection in doctrine or practice, in any church in that confederation, or any part in any such church, is ground sufficient for an association to withdraw from such a church or party so deviating or making defection, and exclude such from them in formal manner, and to advertise all the churches in their confederation thereof, in order that all the churches in confederation may withdraw from such in all acts of church communion, to the end that they may be ashamed, and that all the churches may discountenance such, and bear testimony against the defection. Such withdrawing from a defective or disorderly church, is such as arises from voluntary confederation aforesaid, and not only from the general duty that is incumbent upon all orthodox persons and churches to do, where no such confederation is entered into, as 2 Cor. 16 : 16, 17 ; and although an association ought not to assume a power to excommunicate, or deliver a disorderly or defective church to Satan (as some about us claim), yet it is a power sufficient to exclude the delegates of a disorderly or defective church from an association, and to refuse their presence at their consultations, and advise all the churches in confederation to do so too." *

The benefits arising from an association of churches are many. " In general, it will tend to maintain the truth, order, and discipline of the gospel. 1. By it the churches may have such doubts as arise amongst them cleared, which will prevent disputes. Acts 15 : 28, 29. 2. They will be furnished with salutary counsel. Prov. 11 : 14. 3. Those churches which have no ministers may obtain occasional supplies. Cant. 8 : 8. 4. The churches will be more closely united in promoting the cause

---

* Power and Duty of an Association, by Rev. B. Griffith, adopted by the Philadelphia and Charleston Associations.

and interest of Christ. 5. A member who is aggrieved through partiality, or any other wrongs received from the church, may have an opportunity of applying for direction. 6. A godly and sound ministry will be encouraged, while a ministry that is unsound and ungodly will be discountenanced. 7. There will be a reciprocal communication of their gifts. Phil. 4 : 15. 8. Ministers may alternately be sent out to preach the gospel to those who are destitute. Gal. 2 : 9. 9. A large party may draw off from the church, by means of an intruding minister, or otherwise, and the aggrieved may have no way of obtaining redress but from the association. 10. A church may become heretical, with which its godly members can no longer communicate; yet can obtain no relief but by the association. 11. Contentions may arise betwixt churches, which the association is most likely to remove. 12. The churches may have candidates for the ministry properly tried by the association." *

Conventions are composed of delegates from associations, churches, and other religious bodies. The

---

* Summary of Church Discipline, ch. vi. published by D. Sheppard, in the volume before referred to. Charleston, 1831. On this subject see, also, A Treatise on Church Discipline, in the same volume, ch. x., xi. Griffith's Essay, pp. 231—237. Baptist Confession of Faith, ch. xxvii., § 14, 15. Crowell's Manual, pp. 86, 266. Punchard on Congregationalism, pp. 103, 119. Bacon's Manual, ch. vii. Grantham's Christianismus Primitivus, B. II. ch. x.

general principles upon which they are founded, and the uses which they subserve, are the same as those which obtain in the organization of associations. In this country, a convention is held annually in each of the States, and a general convention is held triennially, consisting of delegates from many States. The latter is an organization for missionary purposes alone, contemplating the introduction of the gospel into destitute regions, and its diffusion throughout the world.

Such is the scriptural relation of churches to each other; such are the confederations which are permitted and sanctioned by the word and the spirit of Christ; and of such alone have we any record in the early annals of Christianity. All other confederations, not deriving their powers from the consent of the churches, and claiming a divine right of jurisdiction over them, are the growth of later and corrupt times. The history of their origin, development, and fearful ascendency, is replete with warning and admonition.*

* Hüllmann Kirchenverfassung, § 31—35. Coleman's Christ. Antiq. pp. 356—367. Prim. Ch. chap. viii. King's Prim. Ch. P. I. chap. viii. Mosheim (Ed. Murdock), I. pp. 86, 142--4. Waddington, Eccl. Hist. p. 44. Gieseler, I. pp. 96, 102, 152.

## CHAPTER XVII.

ADVANTAGES OF SCRIPTURAL CHURCH POLITY.

BEFORE proceeding to enumerate the advantages of the divine plan of ecclesiastical organization and government, I shall present a condensed summary of the principles which have been established in the foregoing investigations. The Scriptures teach that the Christian Church — the Holy Church Catholic — is the spiritual body of the Redeemer, and is composed of those, in every age of the world, who are spiritually renewed, and vitally allied to their Great Head. Some have already ascended to heaven, others are serving him upon earth, and an innumerable multitude are yet to be born. The number will be complete when they are assembled at the judgment seat of Christ. This church universal has its earthly representative, or antitype, in a particular visible church. Each particular church is a local society, composed of persons who have been baptized upon a credible profession of faith in the Son of God, and have solemnly covenanted to walk together in the spirit of the Gospel, acknowledging Christ as their Lord, and his word as their infallible guide. Upon such a church, Christ has conferred the prerogative of self-government, under his laws. It is the right and duty of a church to interpret these laws for itself, and to declare what it considers the will of Christ to be, with reference to doctrines, ordinances, moral duties, the terms of communion, and church order, and to govern all its members accordingly; to receive persons to fellowship and to expel offenders; and to choose its own officers. In the execution of the laws of Christ, it is responsible solely to Him. Churches are therefore independent of each other, so far as coercive interference is concerned; yet they sustain an intimate relationship; are bound to promote, in all lawful ways, each other's welfare; and to unite their efforts in the general advancement of the Redeemer's kingdom. A church when fully organized is furnished with two classes of officers, one of them having special charge of its spiritual interests, the other, of its temporal or secular concerns. In these classes, there is no distinction in grade. All bishops are of equal rank, and so are all deacons.

Such is the scriptural church polity, as adopted by Baptist churches, in opposition to all other existing systems. It differs from all sorts of prelacy, Roman, Oriental, Episcopal, and Wesleyan, by the principle, that all the servants of Christ in the work of the gospel are of equal rank. It is distinguished from Episcopacy and Presbyterianism, by the principle that the only organized church is a particular church, a society of believers, who statedly meet in one place, for the transaction of its business. It, therefore, excludes every such thing as a provincial or national church, the aggregation of churches, and the centralization or consolidation of church power. It is distinguished from all churches established by law, by asking no aid from the civil ruler, and denying to him all right to interfere with its concerns. It differs from these systems by the principle that all church power resides in the church, and not in its officers; and resides in each church directly and originally by virtue of the voluntary compact of its members, under its divine charter. In fine, it is distinguished from all other systems by the principle that every individual is personally responsible for his religious acts and exercises, that no infant is born a member of the church, nor can be made such by any ecclesiastical rite, personal piety being insisted on as an indispensable qualification for membership.

In our estimate of the advantages of scriptural church polity, it is necessary to distinguish between the legitimate tendencies of the system and its actual results. As the gospel contemplates the perfect holiness of its possessors, but, in consequence of the deep-seated depravity of the human heart, never accomplishes it in the present life, so the direct tendencies of the divine plan of church order are retarded and counterworked by other influences, which prevent their complete development, in the actual condition of the churches. An approximation to the high standard of the Scriptures is all that can reasonably be expected.*

I. The scriptural church polity effects an entire separation between the church and the world, the regenerate and the unregenerate. By its requisition of personal piety in all who approach its ordinances and enjoy its special privileges, it gives to the household of faith a distinctive character, and makes it a witness for God, in the midst of a world lying in wickedness. Had the true principles of church polity been universally recognized, no ecclesiastical establishments would ever have existed, empowered by the civil magistrate to subjugate the conscience, and employing pains and penalties to enforce the reception of its dogmas. The spiritual despotism of pampered hierarchies would have been unknown,

* This obvious principle furnishes a satisfactory reply to all such special pleading as is found in Marshall's Notes on Episcopacy, chapter V. It might be easily shown that the Church of England, of which this writer is so strenuous an advocate, is, in the language of one of her own sons, "the child of regal and aristocratical selfishness and unprincipled tyranny, and bears and has ever borne the marks of her birth." Dr. Arnold. Life and Correspondence, p. 478. Appleton & Co., New York.

and the gospel would have been left free to achieve its triumphs by its own sublime and incomparable power. Christ's kingdom is not of this world. His churches ask nothing of the civil ruler but what every citizen, Jew or Gentile, may lawfully claim — protection in the just exercise of their rights and privileges. They have no right to invoke the aid of government to sustain the distinctive institutions, rites, or doctrines of Christianity. Legal compulsion, in reference to the affairs of the soul, besides being absurd, is an impious invasion of the supremacy of the Most High, and the worst form which human tyranny can assume.*

II. Another advantage of the scriptural form of church government is, that it promotes general intelligence among the members of the church.

Where the government of a church is entrusted to one, or to a select portion of its members, the rest feel relieved of all responsibility; but where all are interested, and are solemnly charged with the management of its concerns, all must appreciate their obligation to study the word of God, devoutly and carefully, that they may become familiar with the great principles by which they are to be guided. The consciousness of occupying so solemn and dignified a position, cannot but exert the happiest

---

* Haldane, Social Worship, chap. XIV.

influence on the mind. When it is remembered by the servant of the Lord Jesus, that it is his high privilege to share, directly, in the reception of members into the church, the exercise of discipline, the choice of officers, and everything else that affects the prosperity of the Redeemer's kingdom, he has the strongest possible inducement to prepare himself for the proper performance of his duties. This is one of the most valuable peculiarities of our polity. Other forms may be expected to secure these advantages only in proportion as they approach the scriptural standard.

III. Scriptural church polity is best fitted to maintain the purity of the churches.

It is readily granted that the freedom of our government — the right of the people to choose their own pastors, and in every other respect to manage their own ecclesiastical affairs, — demands an aggregate of wisdom and piety greater than is needed under other forms. But it must be remembered that the scriptural church polity involves a scriptural constituency. The members of a church become such, only after an entire moral transformation. They profess to have been born again, taught by the Spirit of God, and brought into subjection to his will. Genuine piety in the mass of the members constitutes the surest pledge of purity, and the most effectual rampart against false doctrine, heresy, and general corruption. There is much less danger that the majority of the church will become unsound, than that a few men, claiming to be their authoritative guides, will swerve from the faith.

IV. It best secures the rights of individual members.

Should a member be aggrieved by any of his brethren, whether private or official, he may apply for redress to the church. He is not subject to the control, nor liable to suffer from the caprice, of any irresponsible power. Trial by jury is justly regarded as the palladium of personal rights. In a Christian church, a member, when arraigned upon any charge, enjoys the benefit of trial by a jury of his peers, composed of all his fellow-members. There is, therefore, every reason to expect an impartial verdict.

V. Another advantage of the scriptural polity is found in the motives which it suggests to diligence, activity, and fidelity in the ministry.

The direct accountability of rulers to the people is a principle of vast importance, and its beneficial influence is clearly recognized in the best forms of civil government. An officer of the church is amenable to his brethren for the proper discharge of the duties of his station. Should he become negligent, indolent, heretical, or corrupt, he may be deposed. He cannot continue, as under some other systems, to be an incubus to the church, and a scandal to the cause of Christ.

VI. Scriptural church polity is favorable to human progress, — to the establishment of free institutions.

It recognizes distinctly the democratic principle, that the people are the source of power — the fountain of all legitimate authority — while, at the same time, it guards against its abuses, by the limitations of a written constitution. The church does not interfere with the state, it enjoins obedience to rulers, and may exist under any form of civil government; but it cannot be denied that the spirit which pervades its polity is eminently conducive to the political welfare of mankind, and the general advancement of free principles. A people thoroughly imbued with the spirit of our ecclesiastical organization, republicans in church as well as state, will be faithful guardians of the public weal, and every church will prove a citadel of defence against tyranny. The intimate relation which subsists between ecclesiastical and civil freedom is too often overlooked. They are twin sisters, and live or die together. He who surrenders his religious rights to the clergy, or commits the keeping of his conscience to them, and submits to be ruled by them, whether in councils or conferences, renounces his Christian birth-right, and, as he has become the voluntary slave of a priest, he may, at any time, be made the vassal of a tyrant.\*

VII. Another striking feature of the system which I have delineated from the word of God, and the last that I shall mention, is its simplicity.

It presents no imposing visible organization, recognizes no priesthood clothed with mysterious powers; symbolizes with none of the superstitions of the world, " gay religions, full of pomp and gold." The principles of church polity are level to the comprehension of all who are qualified for membership in a church. There are no wheels within wheels, inferior and superior courts of judicature, no intricate machinery, nothing in the government of a church which a plain man may not understand. Its practicability, under any circumstances, is one of its best recommendations.†

---

\* "I am convinced," says Dr. Arnold, "that the whole mischief of the great anti-christian apostacy has for its root the tenet of a priestly government transmitted by a mystical succession from the apostles." Life, p. 320. Again, "That the church system, or rather the priest system, is not to be found in the Scriptures, is as certain as that the worship of Jupiter is not the doctrine of the gospel." p. 409.

† The limits to which I proposed to confine myself, in this chapter, permitted nothing beyond a cursory glance at some of the advantages of the revealed polity. For a more extensive view of the subject, the reader is referred to Punchard on Congregationalism, Part V. Haldane's Social Worship, chap. XIII. Christian Review, May, 1846.

The following anecdote was communicated to the Christian Watchman several years ago, by the Rev. Dr. Fishback, of Lexington, Ky.

"Mr. Editor. — The following circumstance which occurred in the state of Virginia, relative to Mr. Jefferson, was detailed to me by Elder Andrew Tribble, about six years ago, who since died when ninety-two or three years old. The facts may interest some of your readers. Andrew Tribble was the pastor of a small Baptist church, which held its monthly meetings at a short distance from Mr. Jefferson's house, eight or ten years before the American revolution. Mr. Jefferson attended the meetings of the church for several months in succession, and after one of them, asked Elder Tribble to go home and dine with him, with which he complied.

"Mr. Tribble asked Mr. Jefferson how he was pleased with their church government. Mr. Jefferson replied, that it had struck him with great force, and had interested him much; that he considered it the only form of *pure democracy* that then existed in the world, and had concluded that it would be the *best plan of government for the American colonies*. This was several years before the Declaration of Independence, To what extent this practical exhibition of religious liberty and equality operated on Mr. Jefferson's mind, in forming his views and principles of religious and civil freedom, which were so ably exhibited, I will not say."

## CHAPTER XVIII.

#### CORRUPTION OF SCRIPTURAL CHURCH POLITY.

The simple and beautiful system of ecclesiastical polity which was established by the inspired founders of the primitive churches, retained only for a brief period its original perfection and symmetry. The innovations and corruptions which menaced it were distinctly foreseen by the apostles themselves. Paul said to the elders of the church of Ephesus, " I know this, that after my departing shall grievous wolves enter in among you, not sparing the flock."* John encountered the opposition of one of these disturbers of the peace, in the person of Diotrephes, who was so inflamed with the passion for preëminence that he rejected the authority of the apostle himself.† Thus we find the germs of corruption existing even in the primitive churches. To anticipate their development and counteract their insidious influence, the apostles lifted their voices in solemn warning and remonstrance. Notwithstanding this, the churches began to decline from the apostolic order before the close of the second century, and

\* Acts 20 : 29.
† 3 Jno. 9; cf. Clem. Ep. ad Cor. § 14.

even within the lifetime of some who had been contemporary with the inspired teachers. The causes and the manner of this transition will now be briefly indicated. While the early corruptions of church polity are to be ascribed mainly to the pride and ambition of the clergy, it must be confessed that other causes contributed to these deplorable results.

I. The excellences by which the primitive pastors were distinguished, proved one of the earliest occasions of corruption to the churches.

The position of a Christian pastor, in those days, was one of great peril. In all persecutions for the truth's sake, the storm spent its fury chiefly upon him; and the steadfastness with which he endured its violence, entitled him to the love and confidence of his flock. To such men, who were ready to lay down their lives for the cause of Christ, the churches naturally supposed that they might entrust their dearest rights. Their members, scattered by persecution, and prevented from meeting together for the management of their ecclesiastical affairs, were induced by the necessity of the case to commit them to the hands of their pastors, and thus an unscriptural authority was given to religious teachers. This authority was, doubtless, at first faithfully exercised, and held as a boon, not as a right; but, in the course of time, the origin and nature of the trust were overlooked, and their ambitious successors claimed a divine right to dictate to the churches and control their movements. The tendency of power to pass from the many to the few, is strong under any circumstances; but it is particularly so, when the transfer is prompted by reverence for elevated piety, and gratitude for distinguished services. This was the case with the early churches. The lamentable consequences of their defection should prove a warning to all other churches, and impress them with the importance of guarding their rights against the aggression of even the most wise and pious men. Clerical despotism reaches its imperial elevation by slow and almost imperceptible advances; it is the first step that is the most dangerous.

The sentiment of respect for superior excellence, to which I have adverted, led, also, to a change in the relations of the ministers among themselves. "After the death of the apostles and the pupils of the apostles, to whom the general direction of the churches had always been conceded, some one amongst the presbyters of each church was suffered gradually to take the lead in its affairs. In the same irregular way the title of bishop was appropriated to this first presbyter." *

II. Another cause of the corruption of the apostolic church polity is found in the ascendency

---

* Gieseler, Ch. Hist. 1, § 2. Hüllmann, S. 20.

of the churches in the cities over those in the country.

The gospel was first preached in large cities such as Jerusalem, Corinth, and Rome; churches were founded in them, and thence, as from centres of influence, Christianity was extended in the surrounding regions. Visitants to the city were converted, and connected with the metropolitan church; and, in process of time, when their number became sufficiently large, they were constituted into churches in the country. These churches naturally looked to the mother church for aid and counsel, received their first pastors from it, and were in constant intercourse with it. They were regarded as branches of the metropolitan church. "In this connection and coalition, between the original church and the smaller ones that sprang up around it, began that change in the original organization of the apostolical churches which gave rise to the Episcopal system, and which in the end totally subverted the primitive simplicity and freedom in which the churches were at first founded." *

When the elders of the city churches came to have a president, or chief presbyter, charged with the general supervision of its affairs, his jurisdiction was extended over the country churches connected with it; and in this way diocesan episcopacy was

* Coleman, Prim. Ch. p. 249. Gieseler, I, p. 103. Hüllmann, S. 22, 30.

introduced. Had the independence of the rural churches been maintained, this defection from primitive episcopacy could never have occurred.

III. The original polity of the churches was corrupted by the introduction of the doctrine that the ministers of the Christian church were the successors of the Jewish priesthood.

If this notion were true, of course the Christian ministry and the Jewish priesthood must be similar in rank and station. The bishop corresponded to the High Priest, the presbyters or elders to the priests, and the deacons to the Levites. They were no longer incumbents in office at the pleasure of the people, and dependent upon them, but were divinely appointed to instruct and rule them. "When once the idea of a Mosaic priesthood had been adopted in the Christian church, the clergy soon began to assume a superiority over the laity. The customary form of consecration was now supposed to have a certain mystic influence, and henceforth they stand in the position of persons appointed by God to be the medium of communication between him and the Christian world." * This unscriptural and impious dogma was the source of that ghostly tyranny which presumed to extend its empire over heaven and hell, opening or shutting their gates at pleasure, and by its subsequent ascendency kept the

* Gieseler, I, p. 156. Münscher, Handbuch, iii. S. 15.

Christian world for centuries in a worse than Egyptian bondage.\*

Another effect of this doctrine was the claim on the part of the clergy to tithes for their support. Moreover, they argued that "if the ministration of condemnation be glory, much more doth the ministration of righteousness exceed in glory"— and therefore claimed superior contributions in tithes and offerings to Christian ministers. "And what is still more extraordinary, by such wretched reasoning the bulk of mankind were convinced." †

IV. The institution of provincial synods, and afterwards of general councils, contributed its influence to the subversion of the primitive polity of the churches.

The first of these assemblies was held against the Montanists. ‡ They were composed originally of the representatives of independent churches, selected for the purpose of deliberating upon matters which affected their common interests. From these synods the laity was excluded; at least there exists no evidence to prove that any but the clergy took part in their deliberations. They were advisory

---

\* Some Protestant ministers in this country, arrayed in gown or surplice, gravely pretend to these awful prerogatives. Risum teneatis, amici?

† Campbell, Lec. Eccl. Hist. X, P. I. Gibbon's Rome, I. p. 276.

‡ A. D. 160, 170. Euseb. V. 16. Gieseler, 1, p. 102.

bodies, and if their decisions assumed the form of laws, it was rather by common consent than as imperative enactments. It was not long, however, before they presumed to claim the right of giving authoritative laws to the churches. Their original character, as deliberative and advisory assemblies, was exchanged for one of higher pretensions, claiming legislative and judicial authority, and thus invading the independence of the churches.

These synods needed a moderator; and as they were usually held in the capital of the province, the presiding officer of the city church was commonly chosen. The position, which was at first yielded to him from a spirit of courtesy, was afterward claimed as an official right. The institution of these assemblies thus promoted at once the aggrandizement of the clergy in general, and the exaltation of one in each province to a position of vast and irresponsible power. "The practical effect of these councils, from the beginning, was to give increasing consideration and influence to the clergy, which continually increased, until it finally ended in the full establishment of the ecclesiastical hierarchy."\*

The history of these ecclesiastical assemblies evinces that it is not without reason that the movements

---

\* Coleman, Chr. Antiq. p. 364. Prim. Ch. chap. viii. Waddington, Ch. Hist. pp. 43—45. Gibbon, Rome, I. p. 274. Gieseler, I, § 66.

of similar bodies, at the present day, are watched with jealous solicitude. Associations and conventions ought to be restricted within their appropriate limits, as advisory and executive bodies. Any attempt on their part to invade the independence of the churches, by controlling their faith or practice, or assuming the supervision of matters which have not been entrusted to them, should be promptly and steadfastly resisted.

V. The doctrine of a visible church catholic may be enumerated among the causes which subverted the primitive ecclesiastical order.

This notion, which was early developed, necessarily blended the churches together under a uniform organization, which required a visible head, and led directly to the establishment of the papacy. To maintain uniformity, the central representative of sovereignty must be clothed with unlimited power over every portion of the vast confederation.* That this doctrine is a misconception of the notion of Christian unity, and is unsupported by the word of God, has already been shown.†

---

\* Gieseler, I, §§ 49, 66, 82. Coleman, Prim. Ch. p. 270.

† "There is," says Dr. Arnold, "a *societas generis humani*, and a *societas hominum Christianorum*, but there is not one *respublica* or *civitas* of either, but a great many. The Roman Catholics say there is but one *respublica*, and therefore, with perfect consistency, they say that there must be one central government."—Life, p 166.

VI. The introduction of infant baptism was another cause of the corruption of church polity.

The grounds upon which this rite was introduced, by identifying it with regeneration, and making it essential to salvation, placed it in direct antagonism to the genius of Christianity. Besides imparting increased potency to the cause of corruption, which was already in existence, it exercised a direct and powerful influence upon the churches, and, in the end, effected an entire revolution in their polity. After its introduction, the churches were no longer composed of believers who had been baptised upon profession of their faith in the Redeemer; the distinction between real and nominal Christianity was obliterated: forms and ceremonies usurped the place of vital godliness; Christianity itself was virtually repealed; and the pure and benign system of Jesus of Nazareth degenerated into a profane and cruel superstition.

# ADDENDA.

[The following paragraphs, which ought to have been inserted at the close of Chap. VII., were accidentally omitted :]

If it be the duty of each church, as a separate and independent body, to bear its unequivocal testimony to the truth, it is equally so when it is united with others. A union of churches upon grounds that permit the rejection of principles which each is separately pledged to sustain, is an absurdity so gross and palpable, that it is surprising it should find any advocates. It has indeed been said that "uniformity is not to be secured and preserved by confederacies of churches, confessions of faith, or written codes or formularies framed by man, as bonds of union for the churches of Christ."\* To this it may be replied, that while it is true that the recognition of a common confession does not always secure real uniformity, and this will always be the case, so long as deceivers exist who are base enough to profess what they do not believe, yet this method affords the nearest ap-

---

\* Gospel Developed, By W. B. Johnson, D. D. p. 200.

proximation which can be made to so desirable a result. Real uniformity can exist only among those who "all speak the same thing, and are perfectly joined together in the same mind and in the same judgment." 1 Cor. 1 : 10. A union of contradictions is an impossibility. Agreement in sentiment is the bond of Christian union. "I have heard a great deal," says the judicious Fuller, "of union without sentiment; but I can neither feel nor perceive any such thing, either in myself or others. All the union that I can feel or perceive arises from a similarity of views and pursuits." All other grounds of union are impracticable and worthless, and all the hopes of ecclesiastical prosperity or denominational enlargement which are based upon them will prove deceptive in the end. "Christian enlargement is not accomplished by extending our connections, but by confining them to persons with whom we can have fellowship, communion, concord, and a mutual participation of spiritual interests "\*

\* Fuller's Works, II. pp. 657, 659. Bacon's Manual, App. A. For a further vindication of written articles of faith, the reader is referred to Crowell's Ch. Mem. Manual, pp. 71, 118, and especially to the able essays of Andrew Fuller, on creeds and subscriptions, and similar topics. Works, II. p. 629, seq. In a work entitled "Social Religion Exemplified, by Rev. M. Maurice," p. 64, I find the following brief statement of the ends subserved by a confession of faith : —

If the views which have now been presented with reference to the rights and powers of Christian churches be correct, they are placed in a position of great eminence and responsibility. All the authority which Christ has not reserved to himself, he has delegated to them. They are the guardians of his cause upon the earth. To them he has committed a solemn and responsible trust. It is their imperative duty to retain it in their own hands, and discharge the duties involved in it, with a zeal and fi-

"Since the Bible is allowed to be the only rule of faith and practice, and a very sufficient one, what need was there of a confession of faith and a church covenant? It is replied: 1. The *apostolic* churches had something similar, called *the principles of the oracles of God*, and *the form of sound words*. 2. Persons may in *general* subscribe to the Bible, who at the same time do not believe its contents, as the *Sadducees* of old respecting the five books of *Moses*, with all ancient and modern *heretics*. 3. A collection of the first principles of the oracles of God, is of *great use*, that in their light, as truths of the greatest importance, other things that offer themselves may be tried. 4. This is no *imposition*, because *all* men have an equal right to collect from scripture what they apprehend to be the principles of faith. 5. An *explicit* declaration of our principles is honest and generous. 6. Fundamental principles, collected into one consistent view, appear with stronger evidence, and make deeper impressions. A constellation gives a clearer light than dispersed stars. 7. The various *heresies* in the world make it necessary there should be confessions of faith, *that they which are approved may be made manifest.*"

delity proportionate to the honors and privileges it confers. The fact itself is a noble and affecting appeal to their best sentiments, and it should be the aim of the churches to vindicate the wisdom of the Redeemer in their organization, by proving that the trust has not been bestowed in vain.

# A
# Biographical Sketch
# of
# J. L. Reynolds
# (1812-1877)

## by
## John Franklin Jones

# A BIOGRAPHICAL SKETCH OF J. L. REYNOLDS (1812-1877)

J.L. Reynolds was born March 17, 1812 in Charleston, South Carolina. He graduated first in his class at Charleston College and took full course at Newton Theological Seminary (Cathcart).

He returned to Columbia, South Carolina to pastor. Later, he became the president of Georgetown College, Kentucky. He moved to become the pastor of the Second Baptist Church, Richmond, Virginia (Cathcart).

Reynolds became professor of Latin at South Carolina College and taught there for nearly twenty- five years. At his own request, he transferred to the chair of Moral Philosophy (Cathcart).
At the post-Civil War political changes and the dismissal of the entire faculty in 1874, he became Professor of Latin at Furman University. He served there until his death December 19, 1877. His wife survived him only a short time (Cathcart).

The Campbellite and anti-mission controversies plagued the Baptists in the post-Civil war era. Reynolds was active in that controversy and argued that valid baptism required a biblically- authorized church, substantiating his argument by demonstrating same historically (*Index*, cited by Christian).

## JOHN FRANKLIN JONES

Reynolds' published works included several books: *The Kingdom of Christ in Its Internal and External Development* (1846); *Church Polity: or the Kingdom of Christ, in Its Internal and External Development* (1849); *Southern Graded Series. Reynolds' New Southern Pictorial Reader, Fifth, for Schools and Families* (1869); *Reynolds New Pictorial Reader for Schools and Families* (1870); and *Reynolds' Pictorial Primer* (1871) (Starr).

His pamphlets included "Protestant Republicanism the Conservative Element of American Freedom" (1841); and "Defense of the Circular Letter of the Bethel Association" (1842). His published sermons and addresses included "A Discourse Delivered at the Furman Theological Institution, May 11, 1841 . . . in Consequence of the Death of General William Henry Harrison" (1841); "Inaugural Discourse Delivered before the Board of Trustees of the Furman Institution . . . Dec. 11, 1841" (1842); and "The Man of Letters; Address before the Literary Societies of Wake Forest College North Carolina, June 14, 1849" (1849) (Starr).

## BIBLIOGRAPHY

Cathcart, William, ed. *The Baptist Encyclopaedia: A Dictionary of the Doctrines, Ordinances, Usages, Confessions of Faith, Sufferings, Labors, and Successes, and of the General History of the Baptist Denomination in All Lands, with Numerous Biographical Sketches of Distinguished American and Foreign Baptist, and a Supplement.* Philadelphia, Louis H. Everts, 1881; reprint, Paris, AR: Baptist Standard Bearer, 1988. S.v. "Reynolds, J. L., D.D."

*The Christian Index*, May 26 and June 16, 1843; cited by John T. Christian in *A History of the Baptists of the United States From the First Settlement of the Country to the year 1845.* 2 vols. Nashville: Broadman, 1926. 2:437-38.

Christian John T. *A History of the Baptists of the United States From the First Settlement of the Country to the Year*

A BIOGRAPHICAL SKETCH OF J.L. REYNOLDS

*1845.* 2 vols. Nashville: Broadman, 1926.

Starr, Edward C., ed., *A Baptist Bibliography Being a Register of Printed Material By and About Baptists; Including Works Written Against the Baptists.* 24 vols. Chester, PN: American Baptist Historical Society, 1953. S.v. "Reynolds, J. L., 1812-1877."

BY JOHN FRANKLIN JONES
CORDOVA, TENNESSEE
JULY 2004

# THE BAPTIST STANDARD BEARER, INC.

a non-profit, tax-exempt corporation
committed to the Publication & Preservation
of the Baptist Heritage.

CURRENT TITLES AVAILABLE IN
THE BAPTIST *DISTINCTIVES* SERIES

| | |
|---|---|
| KIFFIN, WILLIAM | A Sober Discourse of Right to Church-Communion. Wherein is proved by Scripture, the Example of the Primitive Times, and the Practice of All that have Professed the Christian Religion: That no Unbaptized person may be Regularly admitted to the Lord's Supper. (London: George Larkin, 1681). |
| KINGHORN, JOSEPH | Baptism, A Term of Communion. (Norwich: Bacon, Kinnebrook, and Co., 1816) |
| KINGHORN, JOSEPH | A Defense of "Baptism, A Term of Communion". In Answer To Robert Hall's Reply. (Norwich: Wilkin and Youngman, 1820). |
| GILL, JOHN | Gospel Baptism. A Collection of Sermons, Tracts, etc., on Scriptural Authority, the Nature of the New Testament Church and the Ordinance of Baptism by John Gill. (Paris, AR: The Baptist Standard Bearer, Inc., 2006). |

| | |
|---|---|
| **CARSON, ALEXANDER** | Ecclesiastical Polity of the New Testament. (Dublin: William Carson, 1856). |
| **BOOTH, ABRAHAM** | A Defense of the Baptists. A Declaration and Vindication of Three Historically Distinctive Baptist Principles. Compiled and Set Forth in the Republication of Three Books. Revised edition. (Paris, AR: The Baptist Standard Bearer, Inc., 2006). |
| **BOOTH, ABRAHAM** | Paedobaptism Examined on the Principles, Concessions, and Reasonings of the Most Learned Paedobaptists. With Replies to the Arguments and Objections of Dr. Williams and Mr. Peter Edwards. 3 volumes. (London: Ebenezer Palmer, 1829). |
| **CARROLL, B. H.** | *Ecclesia* - The Church. With an Appendix. (Louisville: Baptist Book Concern, 1903). |
| **CHRISTIAN, JOHN T.** | Immersion, The Act of Christian Baptism. (Louisville: Baptist Book Concern, 1891). |
| **FROST, J. M.** | Pedobaptism: Is It From Heaven Or Of Men? (Philadelphia: American Baptist Publication Society, 1875). |
| **FULLER, RICHARD** | Baptism, and the Terms of Communion; An Argument. (Charleston, SC: Southern Baptist Publication Society, 1854). |
| **GRAVES, J. R.** | Tri-Lemma: or, Death By Three Horns. The Presbyterian General Assembly Not Able To Decide This Question: "Is Baptism In The Romish Church Valid?" 1st Edition. |

| | |
|---|---|
| | (Nashville: Southwestern Publishing House, 1861). |
| **MELL, P.H.** | Baptism In Its Mode and Subjects. (Charleston, SC: Southern Baptist Publications Society, 1853). |
| **JETER, JEREMIAH B.** | Baptist Principles Reset. Consisting of Articles on Distinctive Baptist Principles by Various Authors. With an Appendix. (Richmond: The Religious Herald Co., 1902). |
| **PENDLETON, J.M.** | Distinctive Principles of Baptists. (Philadelphia: American Baptist Publication Society, 1882). |
| **THOMAS, JESSE B.** | The Church and the Kingdom. A New Testament Study. (Louisville: Baptist Book Concern, 1914). |
| **WALLER, JOHN L.** | Open Communion Shown to be Unscriptural & Deleterious. With an introductory essay by Dr. D. R. Campbell and an Appendix. (Louisville: Baptist Book Concern, 1859). |

For a complete list of current authors/titles, visit our internet site at:
www.standardbearer.org
or write us at:

## The Baptist Standard Bearer, Inc.

NUMBER ONE IRON OAKS DRIVE • PARIS, ARKANSAS 72855

*TEL # 479-963-3831*          *FAX # 479-963-8083*
*EMAIL: Baptist@centurytel.net*   *http://www.standardbearer.org*

*Thou hast given a standard to them that fear thee; that it may be displayed because of the truth. — Psalm 60:4*

www.ingramcontent.com/pod-product-compliance
Lightning Source LLC
Chambersburg PA
CBHW021806220426
43662CB00006B/203